A TREATISE ON THE VENERATION OF
THE HOLY ICONS WRITTEN IN ARABIC
BY THEODORE ABŪ QURRAH,
BISHOP OF HARRĀN (C.755-C.830 A.D.)

EASTERN CHRISTIAN TEXTS IN TRANSLATION

A TREATISE ON THE VENERATION OF THE HOLY ICONS WRITTEN IN ARABIC BY THEODORE ABŪ QURRAH, BISHOP OF HARRĀN (C.755-C.830 A.D.)

TRANSLATED INTO ENGLISH, WITH INTRODUCTION AND NOTES

BY

By SIDNEY H. GRIFFITH

PEETERS

1997

ISBN 90-6831-928-0 (Peeters Leuven)
D. 1997/0602/37

Imprimerie Orientaliste, s.p.r.l., Louvain (Belgique)

TABLE OF CONTENTS

FOREWORD

With this book, Peeters Press inaugurates the series, "Eastern Christian Texts in Translation." This new collection will make available to readers, in a continuing series, a variety of documents translated into English from the major language-groups of early Christianity in the East: Arabic, Armenian, Coptic, Georgian, Ethiopic, Greek and Syriac. Published in conjunction with the *Corpus Scriptorum Christianorum Orientalium* (*CSCO*), it will present many of the texts which received their first critical editions in that series.

Since its inception in 1903, the *CSCO* has aimed to provide scholars with texts from eastern Christian churches. The *Corpus* was to embrace all literary productions coming from Christian milieux in the Near East in the ancient and medieval periods, and texts were to be accompanied by an introduction, explanatory notes and a translation. Even though the presentation of a translation in a modern language — not to mention Latin versions — was considered a requirement, because translating is an inseparable part of the task of a text editor, the focus was on the critically edited text. The wise directorships of the founders of the *Corpus*, J.-B. Chabot and H. Hyvernat, followed by R. Draguet and the late A. de Halleux, maintained and gradually enhanced the philological quality of the volumes, making the *CSCO* the largest collection of Christian oriental texts. It will continue as before.

A growing interest among a broader public in the sources and traditions of eastern Christianity has made it opportune to provide readers with easily available and scientifically sound translations. The Editor and the Board of the *CSCO* supported the idea for such a collection, considering it to combine two goals: to continue addressing an audience of scholars, on the one hand; and to answer the need of an ever more interested public, on the other.

"Eastern Christian Texts in Translation" is not another series inside the *CSCO*; rather, it will constitute a new collection in conjunction with the *Corpus*. The latter brings its long experience in publishing Christian oriental texts with their translations — a tradition fulfilling the highest scientific criteria — as well as a huge deposit of texts, some of which will now become more widely known through a modern and vivid retranslation.

The Board of "Eastern Christian Texts in Translation" is composed of well-known specialists in the field of Christian oriental literatures, who will make the undertaking a success. To them, the *CSCO* addresses its most sincere encouragement.

Bernard Coulie,
Editor, *Corpus Scriptorum Christianorum Orientalium*

ABBREVIATIONS

AASS   = *Acta Sanctorum* (71 vols.; Paris 1863-1940).
CSCO   = *Corpus Scriptorum Christianorum Orientalium*
EI   = *The Encyclopedia of Islam* (4 vols.; Leiden & London, 1913-1934; new edition; Leiden & London, 1960-   ).
GCAL = G. Graf, *Geschichte der christlichen arabischen Literatur* (5 vols.; Studi e Testi, 118, 133, 146, 147, 172; Città del Vaticano, 1944-1953).
Mansi = G.D. Mansi, *Sacrorum Conciliorum Nova et Amplissima Collectio* (53 vols. in 58 pts.; Paris & Leipzig, 1901-1927).
PAC   = *Patrimoine arabe chrétien*
PG   = J.-P. Migne (ed.), *Patrologia Cursus Completus, Series Graeca* (161 vols. in 166 pts.; Paris, 1857-1866).
SC   = *Sources chrétiennes*
TU   = *Texte und Untersuchungen zur Geschichte der altchristlichen Literatur*

BIBLIOGRAPHY

P.J. ALEXANDER, *The Patriarch Nicephorus of Constantinople; Ecclesiastical Policy and Image Worship in the Byzantine Empire* (Oxford, 1958).
D. ANDERSON (trans.), *St. John of Damascus, On the Divine Images: Three Apologies against Those Who Attack the Holy Images* (Crestwood, N.Y., 1980).

J. ARENDZEN, *Theodori Abū Kurra De cultu imaginum libellus a codice Arabico nunc primum editus Latine versus illustratus* (Bonn, 1897).

J.S. ASSEMANUS, *Bibliotheca Orientalis Clementino-Vaticana ...* (3 vols. in 4; Romae, 1719-1728).

M.-F. AUZÉPY, "De la Palestine à Constantinople (VIIIᵉ-IXᵉ siècles): Étienne le Sabaïte et Jean Damascène," *Travaux et Mémoires* 12 (1994), 183-218.

C. BACHA, *Les œuvres arabes de Théodore Aboucara, évêque de Haran* (Beyrouth, 1904).

C. BACHA, *Un traité des œuvres arabes de Théodore Abou-Kurra, évêque de Harran; publié et traduit en français pour la première fois* (Tripoli de Syrie & Rome, 1905).

A. BADAWI, *La transmission de la philosophie grecque au monde arabe* (Etudes de Philosophie Médiévale, 56; Paris, 1968).

M. AL-BAKHĪT & R. SCHICK (eds.), *The Fifth International Conference on the History of Bilād al-Shām during the Abbasid Period* (English Section; Amman, 1991).

M. AL-BAKHĪT & R. SCHICK (eds.), *The Fourth International Conference on the History of Bilād al-Shām during the Umayyad Period, Proceedings of the Third Symposium* (English Section; Amman, 1989).

G. BARDY, *Eusèbe de Césarée, Histoire Ecclésiastique; livres V-VII* (SC, no. 41; Paris, 1955).

G. BARDY, "La littérature patristique des 'Quaestiones et Responsiones,' sur l'écriture sainte," *Revue Biblique* 42 (1933), 328-332.

S. BASHEAR, "Qibla Musharriqa and Early Muslim Prayer in Churches," *The Muslim World* 81 (1991), 267-282.

N.H. BAYNES, "The Icons Before Iconoclasm," *Harvard Theological Review* 44 (1951), 93-106.

R.P. BLAKE, "Catalogue des manuscrits géorgiens de la bibliothèque de la laure d'Iviron au mont Athos," *Revue de l'Orient Chrétien* 23, 3rd. ser., 8 (1931-1932), 324-325.

M.J. BLANCHARD, "The Georgian Version of the Martyrdom of Saint Michael, Monk of Mar Sabas Monastery." Forthcoming in *ARAM* 6 [1997].

J. BLAU, *A Grammar of Christian Arabic* (CSCO, vols. 267, 276, 279; Louvain, 1966-1967).

J. BLAU, "The Influence of Living Aramaic on Ancient South Palestinian Christian Arabic," in his *Studies in Middle Arabic and its Judaeo-Arabic Variety* (Jerusalem, 1988), 288-290.

J. BLAU, "A Melkite Arabic Literary *Lingua Franca* from the Second Half of the First Millennium," *Bulletin of the School of Oriental and African Studies* 57 (1994), 14-16.

F. BOESPFLUG et N. LOSSKY (eds.), *Nicée II, 787-1987; douze siècles d'images religieuses* (Paris, 1987).

E.A. WALLIS BUDGE, *The History of the Blessed Virgin Mary and the History of the Likeness of Christ* (2 vols.; London, 1899).

Th.A. BUSINK, *Der Tempel von Jerusalem von Salomo bis Herodes; eine archäologisch-historische Studie unter Berücksichtigung des westsemitischen Tempelbaus* (2 vols.; Leiden, 1970 & 1980).

C. CAHEN, *La Syrie du nord à l'époque des croisades et la principauté franque d'Antioche* (Bibliothèque orientale, t. 1; Paris, 1940).

A. CAMERON, "The History of the Image of Edessa; the Telling of a Story," in *Okeanos; Essays Presented to Ihor Sevcenko, Harvard Ukrainian Studies* 7 (1983), 80-94.

M. CANARD, "*Da'wa*," *EI*, new edition, Vol. II, 168-170.

J.-B. CHABOT, *Anonymi Auctoris Chronicon ad A.C. 1234 Pertinens* (CSCO, vols. 81, 82, 109, 354; Louvain, 1916, 1920, 1937 & 1974).

J.-B. CHABOT, *Chronique de Michel le Syrien; patriarche jacobite d'Antioche (1166-1199). Editée pour la première fois et traduite en français* (4 vols.; Paris, 1899-1910).

L. CHEIKHO, et al. (eds.), *Eutychii Patriarchae Alexandrini Annales* (CSCO, vol. 51; Beirut, 1909).

K. CORRIGAN, *Visual Polemics in the Ninth-Century Byzantine Psalters* (Cambridge & New York, 1992).

P. CRONE, "Islam, Judeo-Christianity and Byzantine Iconoclasm," *Jerusalem Studies in Arabic and Islam* 2 (1980) 59-95.

A. DI BERARDINO (ed.), *Encyclopedia of the Early Church* (2 vols.; Cambridge, 1992).

I. DICK, "Un continuateur arabe de saint Jean Damascène: Théodore Abuqurra, évêque melkite de Harrān," *Proche Orient Chrétien* 12 (1961), 209-223, 319-332; 13 (1963), 114-129.

I. DICK, "Deux écrits inédits de Théodore Abūqurra," *Le Muséon* 72 (1959), 53-67.

I. DICK, "La passion arabe de s. Antoine Ruwah, néomartyr de Damas († 25 déc. 799)," *Le Muséon* 74 (1961), 109-133.

I. DICK, "Thédore Abuqurra évêque melkite de Harran (750?-825?); introduction générale, texte et analyse du traité de l'existence du créateur et de la vraie religion." (unpublished Ph.D. Thesis; Université Catholique de Louvain, Louvain, 1960).

I. DICK, *Théodore Abūqurra, Traité du culte des icônes* (PAC, 10; Rome & Jounieh, 1986).

I. DICK, *Thédore Abūqurra, Traité du culte du Créateur et de la vraie religion. Introduction et texte critique* (PAC 3; Rome & Jounieh, 1982).

E. VON DOBSCHÜTZ, *Christusbilder; Untersuchungen zur christlichen Legende* (TU, vol. XVIII; Leipzig, 1899), 102-196.

L. DUCHESNE, "L'iconographie byzantine dans un document grec du IXe siècle," *Roma e l'Oriente* 5 (1912-1913), 222-239, 273-285, 349-366.

B. DODGE, *The Fihrist of al-Nadim* (2 vols.; New York, 1970).

G. DUMEIGE, *Nicée II* (Histoire des Conciles Oecuméniques, vol. 4; Paris, 1978).

D.M. DUNLOP, *Arab Civilization to A.D. 1500* (London, 1971).

K. DUCHATELEZ, "La notion d'économie et ses richesses théologiques," *Nouvelle Revue Théologique* 92 (1970), 267-308.

J.-M. FIEY, "Image d'Edesse ou linceul de Turin, qu'est-ce qui a été transféré à Constantinople en 944?" *Revue d'Histoire Ecclésiastique* 82 (1987), 271-277.

G. FLÜGEL, *Kitāb al-Fihrist* (New photo-ed.; Beirut, 1964).

M. GALLO, *Palestinese anonimo, Omelia arabo-cristiana dell'VIII secolo. Traduzione, introduzione e note* (Roma, 1994).

M. GAUTIER-VAN BERCHEM, "The Mosaics of the Dome of the Rock in Jerusalem and of the Great Mosque in Damascus," in

K.A.C. Creswell, *Early Muslim Architecture, Umayyads A.D. 622-750* (2nd ed.; Oxford, 1969).

S. GERO, *Byzantine Iconoclasm during the Reign of Constantine V* (CSCO, vol. 384; Louvain, 1977).

A. GRABAR, *Christian Iconography: a Study of its Origins* (Princeton, 1968).

O. GRABAR, "*Kubbat al-Sakhra*," *EI*, new edition, vol. V, 298-299.

G. GRAF, *Die arabischen Schriften des Theodor Abu Qurra, Bischofs von Harrān* (ca. 740-820) (Paderborn, 1910).

G. GRAF, *Die Schriften des Jacobiten Ḥabīb ibn Ḫidma Abū Rāʾiṭa* (CSCO, vols. 130 & 131; Louvain 1951).

S.H. GRIFFITH, "Anthony David of Baghdad, Scribe and Monk of Mar Sabas: Arabic in the Monasteries of Palestine," *Church History* 58 (1989), 7-19.

S.H. GRIFFITH, *Arabic Christianity in the Monasteries of Ninth-Century Palestine* (Collected Studies Series CS380; Aldershot, 1992).

S.H. GRIFFITH, "The Controversial Theology of Theodore Abū Qurrah (c.750-c.820 A.D.); a Methodological, Comparative Study in Christian Arabic Literature." (Ph.D. dissertation, The Catholic University of America, Washington, D.C., 1978).

S.H. GRIFFITH, "Eutychius of Alexandria on the Emperor Theophilus and Iconoclasm in Byzantium: a Tenth Century Moment in Christian Apologetics in Arabic," *Byzantion* 52 (1982), 154-190.

S.H. GRIFFITH, "Faith and Reason in Christian Kalām: Theodore Abū Qurrah on Discerning the True Religion," in S.Kh. Samir and J.S. Nielsen, *Christian Arabic Apologetics during the Abbasid Period (750-1258)* (Studies in the History of Religions, vol. LXIII; Leiden & New York, 1994), 1-43.

S.H. GRIFFITH, "The First Christian Summa Theologiae in Arabic: Christian Kalām in Ninth-Century Palestine," in M. Gervers & R.J. Bikhazi (eds.), *Conversion and Continuity; Indigenous Christian Communities in Islamic Lands, Eighth to Eighteenth Centuries* (Papers in Mediaeval Studies, 9; Toronto, 1990), 15-31.

S.H. GRIFFITH, "Free Will in Christian Kalām: the Doctrine of Theodore Abū Qurrah," *Parole de l'Orient* 14 (1987) 79-107.

S.H. GRIFFITH, "From Aramaic to Arabic; the Languages of the Monasteries of Palestine in the Byzantine and Early Islamic Periods," presented at symposium, "Palestine and Transjordan before Islam," Dumbarton Oaks, Washington, D.C. 28-30, April 1995, forthcoming in *Dumbarton Oaks Papers*.

S.H. GRIFFITH, "Greek into Arabic: Life and Letters in the Monasteries of Palestine in the Ninth Century; the Example of the Summa Theologiae Arabica," *Byzantion* 56 (1986) 117-138.

S.H. GRIFFITH, "Images, Islam and Christian Icons," in P. Canivet & J.-Paul Rey-Coquais (eds.), *La Syrie, de Byzance à l'Islam, VIIᵉ-VIIIᵉ siècles* (Damas, 1992), 121-138.

S.H. GRIFFITH, "Islam and the Summa Theologiae Arabica; Rabiʿ I, 264 A.H.," *Jerusalem Studies in Arabic and Islam* 13 (1990), 225-264.

S.H. GRIFFITH, "Michael, the Martyr and Monk of Mar Sabas Monastery at the Court of the Caliph ʿAbd al-Malik; Christian Apologetics and Martyrology in the Early Islamic Period," forthcoming in ARAM 7 [1997].

S.H. GRIFFITH, "The Monks of Palestine and the Growth of Christian Literature in Arabic," *The Muslim World* 78 (1988), 1-38.

S.H. GRIFFITH, "Muslims and Church Councils; the Apology of Theodore Abū Qurrah," *Studia Patristica* 25 (1993), 270-299.

S.H. GRIFFITH, "Reflections on the Biography of Theodore Abū Qurrah," *Parole de l'Orient* 18 (1993) 143-170.

S.H. GRIFFITH, "Some Unpublished Arabic Sayings Attributed to Theodore Abū Qurrah," *Le Muséon* 92 (1979), 29-35.

S.H. GRIFFITH, "Stephen of Ramlah and the Christian Kerygma in Arabic in Ninth-Century Palestine," *Journal of Ecclesiastical History* 36 (1985), 23-45.

S.H. GRIFFITH, "Theodore Abū Qurrah's Arabic Tract on the Christian Practice of Venerating Images," *Journal of the American Oriental Society* 105 (1984), 53-73.

S. H. GRIFFITH, *Theodore Abū Qurrah: the Intellectual Profile of an Arab Christian Writer of the First Abbasid Century* (The Tel Aviv University Irene Halmos Chair of Arabic Literature Annual Lecture; Tel Aviv, 1992).

S. H. GRIFFITH, "Theodore Abū Qurrah's On the Veneration of the Holy Icons," *The Sacred Art Journal* 13 (1992), 3-19.

Y. HIRSCHFELD, *The Judean Desert Monasteries in the Byzantine Period* (New Haven & London, 1992).

V. GRUMEL, *La Chronologie* (Paris, 1958).

ʿAMR IBN BAHR AL-JĀHIZ, *Kitāb al-Hayawān. [Vol.] I.* (Cairo, 1938).

A. D. KARTSONIS, *Anastasis; the Making of an Image* (Princeton, 1986).

A. P. KAZHDAN & A.-M. TALBOT et al. (eds.), *The Oxford Dictionary of Byzantium* (3 vols.; New York 1991).

M. KELLERMAN-ROST, "Ein pseudo-aristotelischer Traktat über die Tugend," (Unpublished Ph.D. dissertation; Erlangen, 1965).

H. KENNEDY, *The Early Abbasid Caliphate: a Political History* (London, 1981).

G. H. KHOURY, "Theodore Abū Qurrah (c.750-820): Translation and Critical Analysis of his 'Treatise on the Existence of the Creator and on the True Religion'," (Unpublished Ph.D. dissertation, Graduate Theological Union, Berkeley, California, 1991).

G. R. D. KING, "Islam, Iconoclasm, and the Declaration of Doctrine," *Bulletin of the School of Oriental and African Studies* 48 (1985), 267-277.

C. A. KNELLER, "Theodore Abucara über Papstum und Konzilien," *Zeitschrift für katholische Theologie* 34 (1910) 419-427.

B. KOTTER (ed.), *Die Schriften des Johannes von Damaskos. Vol. III, Contra Imaginum Calumniatores Orationes Tres* (Berlin & New York, 1975).

I. KRACKOVSKIJ, "Theodore Abū Kurra in the Muslim Writers of the Ninth-Tenth Centuries," [Russian] *Christianskij Vostok* 4 (1915), 306.

P. KRAUS, "Zu Ibn al-Muqaffaʿ," *Rivista degli Studi Orientali* 14 (1933), 1-20.

M. L. KREHL (ed.), *Le Recueil des traditions mahométanes par Abou Abdallah Mohammed ibn Ismail el-Bokhari* (4 vols.; Leyde, 1862-1908).

J. C. LAMOREAUX, "An Unedited Tract Against the Armenians by Theodore Abū Qurrah," *Le Muséon* 105 (1992), 327-341.

J. LASSNER, *The Shaping of ʿAbbasid Rule* (Princeton, 1980).

C. MANGO, "Greek Culture in Palestine after the Arab Conquest," in G. Cavallo, G. de Gregorio & M. Maniaci (eds.), *Scritture, Libri e Testi nelle Aree Provinciale di Bisanzio* (Spoleto, 1991) 149-160.

G. MONNOT, "Abū Qurrah et la pluralité des religions," *Revue de l'Histoire des Religions* 208 (1991), 49-71.

J. NASRALLAH, "Regard critique sur I. Dick, *Th. Abū Qurrah, De l'existence du Créateur et de la vraie religion*," *Proche Orient Chrétien* 36 (1986), 46-62; 37 (1987), 63-70.

J. NASRALLAH, *Histoire du mouvement littéraire dans l'église melchite du v au xx siècle; contribution à l'étude de la littérature arabe chrétienne. Vol. II, Tome 2, 750-Xs.* (Louvain, 1988).

B. A. NASSIF, ""On the Confirmation of the Law of Moses, the Gospel and Orthodoxy," a Treatise Written in Arabic by Theodore Abū Qurrah, Bishop of Harran (c. 755-c.829); Translation into English, with Introduction and Analysis." (unpub. M.A. thesis; Holy Cross Greek Orthodox School of Theology, Brookline, Mass., 1996).

R. PARET, "Die Entstehungszeit des islamischen bilderverbots," *Kunst des Orients* II (1976/77), 158-181.

J. PATRICH, *Sabas, Leader of Palestinian Monasticism: A Comparative Study in Eastern Monasticism, Fourth to Seventh Centuries* (Dumbarton Oaks Studies, XXXII; Washington, D.C., 1995).

R. PAYNE Smith, *Thesaurus Syriacus* (2 vols.; Oxford, 1879-1901; reprinted, Hildesheim & New York, 1981).

J. PELIKAN, *Imago Dei; the Byzantine Apologia for Icons* (A.W. Mellon Lectures in the Fine Arts, 1987; Princeton, 1990).

G. PERADZE, "An Account of the Georgian Monks and Monasteries in Palestine," *Georgica* 1, 4 & 5 (1937), 181-246.

P. PEETERS, "La passion de s. Michel le Sabaïte," *Analecta Bollandiana* 48 (1930), 65-98.

P. PIZZO (ed. & trans.), *Teodoro Abu Qurrah, Difesa delle icone. Trattato sulla venerazione delle immagini* (Bibl. Vicino Oriente; Milano, 1995).

N. RESCHER, *Al-Farabi's Short Commentary on Aristotle's Prior Analytics* (Pittsburgh, 1963). D. van Reenen, "The Bilderverbot, a New Survey," *Der Islam* 67 (1990), 27-77.

M. RICHARD, *"Apo Phonês," Byzantion* 20 (1950), pp. 191-222.

C. P. ROTH (trans.), *St. Theodore the Studite on the Holy Icons* (Crestwood, N.Y., 1981).

M.-J. ROUET DE JOURNAL, *Jean Moschus, Le Pré Spirituel* (Paris, 1946).

J. RUSKA, "Thābit b. Kurra," *EI*, vol. IV, 770-771.

D.J. SAHAS (ed. & trans.), *Icon and Logos; an Annotated Translation of the Sixth Session of the Seventh Ecumenical Council* (Toronto, 1986).

Kh. SAMIR [Samir Khalil Samir], "Abū Qurrah et les Maronites," *Proche Orient Chrétien* 41 (1991), 25-33.

Kh. SAMIR [Samir Khalil Samir], "La littérature melkite sous les premiers abbasides," *Orientalia Christiana Periodica* 56 (1990), 469-486.

Kh. SAMIR [Samir Khalil], "Note sur les citations bibliques chez Abū Qurrah," *Orientalia Christiana Periodica* 49 (1983), 184-191.

Kh. SAMIR, "Saint Rawh al-Qurašī. Étude d'onomastique arabe et authenticité de sa passion," *Le Muséon* 105 (1992), 343-359.

Kh. SAMIR [Samir Khalil], "La "Somme des aspects de la foi," œuvre de Abū Qurrah?" *Orientalia Christiana Analecta* 226 (1986) 93-121.

Kh. SAMIR [Samir Khalil Samir], "Le traité sur les icônes d'Abū Qurrah mentionné par Eutychius," *Orientalia Christiana Periodica* 58 (1992), 461-474.

Kh. SAMIR, "Yannah dans l'onomastique arabo-copte," *Orientalia Christiana Periodica* 45 (1979), 166-170.

R. SCHICK, *The Christian Communities of Palestine from Byzantine to Islamic Rule; a Historical and Archaeological Study* (Princeton, 1996).

I. Ševčenko, "Constantinople Viewed from the Eastern Provinces in the Middle Byzantine Period," *Harvard Ukrainian Studies* 3-4 (1979-1980), 712-747; reprinted in his *Ideology, Letters and Culture in the Byzantine World* (London, 1982).

H. J. Sieben, "Zur Entwicklung der Konzilsidee, achter Teil; Theodor Abū Qurra (820/5) über 'unfehlbare' Konzilien," *Theologie und Philosophie* 49 (1974), 489-509.

D. Sourdel, *Le vizirat abbaside* (2 vols.; Damascus, 1959-1960).

G. Tchalenko, *Villages antiques de la Syrie du nord, le massif du Bélus à l'époque romaine* (3 vols.; Paris, 1953-1958).

R. W. Thomson, "An Eighth-Century Melkite Colophon from Edessa," *Journal of Theological Studies* 13 (1962), 249-258.

A. Van Roey, *Nonnus de Nisibe, traité apologétique, étude, texte et traduction* (Bibliothèque du Muséon, vol. 21; Louvain, 1948).

A. Vasiliev, "The Iconoclastic Edict of the Caliph Yazid II, A.D. 721," *Dumbarton Oaks Papers* 9-10 (1956), 23-47.

A. Vasiliev, "The Life of St. Theodore of Edessa," *Byzantion* 16 (1944), 165-225.

R. Walzer, "New Light on the Arabic Translation of Aristotle," in *Greek into Arabic; Essays on Islamic Philosophy* (Oriental Studies, 1; Oxford, 1962).

J. Wansbrough, *Quranic Studies; Sources and Methods of Scriptural Interpretation* (London Oriental Series, 31; Oxford, 1977).

A. J. Wensinck, "*Sadjdjāda*," and "*Salāt*," *EI*, vol. IV, 47-51, 102.

A. J. Wensinck, "*Kibla*," *EI*, new edition, vol. V, 83.

INTRODUCTION

John of Damascus, Theodore Studites, and Nicephorus the patriarch of Constantinople, together with the authors of the acts of the seventh ecumenical council, are the writers who the most readily come to mind when one thinks of those who defended the veneration of the holy icons in the Christian church, in the course of the controversies of the eighth and ninth centuries in the Orthodox communities[1]. But there is another writer whose work on the subject belongs in the company of those we have just named. He is Theodore Abū Qurrah, whose Arabic tract on the veneration of the holy icons is herewith presented in English translation.

Theodore Abū Qurrah

Theodore Abū Qurrah (c.755-830) was the Orthodox bishop of Ḥarrān in Mesopotamia, sometime monk of Mar Sabas monastery

---

[1] Selections from their works are now easily available in modern English translations. See D. Anderson (trans.), *St. John of Damascus on the Divine Images* (Crestwood, N.Y., 1980); C. P. Roth (trans.), *St. Theodore the Studite on the Holy Icons* (Crestwood, N.Y., 1981); P. J. Alexander, *The Patriarch Nicephorus of Constantinople; Ecclesiastical Policy and Image Worship in the Byzantine Empire* (Oxford, 1958); D. J. Sahas (ed. & trans.), *Icon and Logos; an Annotated Translation of the Sixth Session of the Seventh Ecumenical Council* (Toronto, 1986).

in the desert of Judea[2], and a religious controversialist whose jour-
neys in defense of his Chalcedonian faith took him from Egypt to
Armenia, and finally back home to Ḥarrān. Intellectually, as one
will easily notice in his tract on the holy icons, Abū Qurrah was
an heir of St. John of Damascus, his fellow monk of Mar Sabas[3].
Whereas John of Damascus was prominent among the last gener-
ations of Greek writers in the Holy Land in early Islamic times,
Theodore Abū Qurrah was the first Orthodox scholar whose
name we know regularly to write Christian theology in Arabic[4].

Theodore Abū Qurrah became famous, precisely because of
his success in the Arabic language. Many years after his death, the
Syrian Orthodox patriarch of Antioch, Michael I (d.1199),
recorded the memory of Abū Qurrah preserved in the non-Chal-
cedonian, Monophysite community, against whom he had
directed much of his polemical writing. Michael wrote of Abū
Qurrah, "Because he was a sophist, and engaged in dialectics with
the pagans (ḥanpê, i.e., the Muslims) and knew the Saracen language, he was an object of wonder to the simple folk[5]".

---

[2] On the biography of Abū Qurrah, see Ignace Dick, "Un continuateur arabe
de saint Jean Damascène: Théodore Abuqurra, évêque melkite de Ḥarrān,"
Proche Orient Chrétien 12 (1961), pp. 209-223, 319-332; 13 (1963), pp. 114-129; J.
Nasrallah, *Histoire du mouvement littéraire dans l'église melchite du v au xx siècle;
contribution à l'étude de la littérature arabe chrétienne (vol. II, tome 2, 750-Xs.;*
Louvain, 1988), pp. 107 ff; Sidney H. Griffith, "Reflections on the Biography of
Theodore Abū Qurrah," *Parole de l'Orient* 18 (1993) 143-170.

[3] On this monastery see now Yizhar Hirschfeld, *The Judean Desert Monasteries in the Byzantine Period* (New Haven & London, 1992); Joseph Patrich, *Sabas,
Leader of Palestinian Monasticism: A Comparative Study in Eastern Monasticism,
Fourth to Seventh Centuries* (Dumbarton Oaks Studies, XXXII; Washington, D.C.,
1995).

[4] For a list and description of Abū Qurrah's works, see Nasrallah, *Histoire du
mouvement littéraire.*

[5] J.-B. Chabot, *Chronique de Michel le Syrien; patriarche jacobite d'Antioche* (4
vols.; Paris, 1899-1910), vol. III, p. 32 (French); vol. IV, pp. 495-496 (Syriac).

In fact, Theodore Abū Qurrah knew the 'Saracen language' so well that he left behind some twenty authentic compositions in Arabic, with a number of other texts attributed to him, because of his fame as a successful author and controversialist[6]. Moreover, there survive in Greek forty-three works attributed to him, which are arguably translations from Arabic. For Abū Qurrah's fame was in large part tied to his 'Arabicity'. He spoke and wrote the language at a time when it was just becoming the cultural language of classical Islamic civilization, as well as the *lingua sacra* of the *Qur'ān* and of the new world religion[7]. It was also the beginning of the period of mass conversions to Islam on the part of the largely Christian populations of the Greek and Syriac-speaking patriarchates of Alexandria, Antioch and Jerusalem in the territories of Mesopotamia, Syria/Palestine, and Egypt[8].

Abū Qurrah's Arabic was not the elegant *faṣāḥah* of the *littérateurs* of his day. It was a colloquial form of the language which scholars today call 'Middle Arabic.' In this respect it was much like the state of the Arabic language one finds in the 'Old South Palestinian' texts which compose the earliest archive of Christian writings in Arabic to survive to modern times. They date from the eighth to the tenth centuries, and they are mostly translations

[6] On Theodore Abū Qurrah's career as a writer see the information in S. H. Griffith, "Reflections on the Biography of Theodore Abū Qurrah,", esp. 163-164. Information about the preservation of Abū Qurrah's works in Arabic, Greek and Georgian, as well as information about his writings in Syriac are collected here as well.

[7] See the remarks of John Wansbrough, *Quranic Studies; Sources and Methods of Scriptural Interpretation* (London Oriental Series, 31; Oxford, 1977), in the chapter, "Origins of Classical Arabic," pp. 85-118.

[8] See S. H. Griffith, "The First Christian Summa Theologiae in Arabic: Christian Kalām in Ninth-Century Palestine," in M. Gervers & R. J. Bikhazi (eds.), *Conversion and Continuity; Indigenous Christian Communities in Islamic Lands, Eighth to Eighteenth Centuries* (Papers in Mediaeval Studies, 9; Toronto, 1990), pp. 15-31.

from Greek and Syriac originals, including the Scriptures and
other early Christian and monastic classics[9]. There are a few original compositions in Arabic among them, including most of the
Arabic works of Theodore Abū Qurrah. And this fact is no small
part of his claim to fame; he was an original writer in Arabic in an
era when most Christian authors living under Islamic rule still
wrote in Greek, Syriac or Coptic. Since he came from Syria it is
no surprise to learn that Abū Qurrah was also a Syriac speaker. In
fact, as more than one scholar has noticed, the influence of the
idiosyncrasies of Syriac is readily apparent in Abū Qurrah's Arabic
diction[10]. Indeed, Abū Qurrah himself wrote a number of works
in his native Syriac, according to his own testimony. In his Arabic
"Treatise on the Death of Christ," in an extended passage of arguments in defense of 'Orthodoxy' against those whom he calls
'Jacobites', he wrote,

> Likewise from the words of the holy fathers, we have adduced every
> sort of example, in thirty tractates which we composed in Syriac as

---

[9] See J. Blau, *A Grammar of Christian Arabic* (CSCO, vols. 267, 276, 279;
Louvain, 1966-1967), vol. 267, pp. 34-36; idem, "A Melkite Arabic Literary
Lingua Franca from the Second Half of the First Millennium," *Bulletin of
the School of Oriental and African Studies* 57 (1994), pp. 14-16. See also S. H.
Griffith, "The Monks of Palestine and the Growth of Christian Literature in
Arabic," *The Muslim World* 78 (1988), pp. 1-28; *idem*, "Anthony David of
Baghdad, Scribe and Monk of Mar Sabas: Arabic in the Monasteries of Pales-
tine," *Church History* 58 (1989), pp. 7-19, idem, "From Aramaic to Arabic; the
Languages of the Monasteries of Palestine in the Byzantine and Early Islamic
Periods," a paper delivered at the symposium on "Palestine and Transjordan
before Islam," Dumbarton Oaks, Washington, D.C. 28-30 April 1995, to
be published with the symposium proceedings in a forthcoming issue of
Dumbarton Oaks Papers.
[10] See Griffith, "The Monks of Palestine and the Growth of Christian Literature in Arabic," p. 11. See too the remarks of Joshua Blau, "The Influence of
Living Aramaic on Ancient South Palestinian Christian Arabic," in J. Blau,
Studies in Middle Arabic and its Judaeo-Arabic Variety (Jerusalem, 1988), pp. 288-
290.

a commendation for the opinion of Orthodoxy and for the declaration of the holy Mar Leo, the bishop of Rome[11].

Nevertheless, he was among the first Christians to exploit the
apologetic potential of the new Arabic medium of public discourse. The marvel is not that he wrote a vulgar or colloquial
form of the language, but that he was writing in Arabic at all.

Theodore Abū Qurrah's career is the exemplar of the new era
in the life of the church in Islamic lands which dawned with the
success of the Abbasid revolution. Historians of Islam have often
pointed to the cultural shift of position which the revolution
effected; the Islamic community turned its back, so to speak, to
the Mediterranean and the world of Byzantium, to face east and
to come under the cultural tutelage of the Persian masters of the
Arabic language[12]. The Christians in the caliphate, and particularly the Melkites, followed suit. In the Christian case, the shift
can be seen in the community's response to the controversy over
the practice of venerating the icons of Christ and the saints.
When the crisis first arose in Umayyad times, and the church in
the Holy Land became alarmed, St. John of Damascus responded
with three orations in Greek, addressed to his own local community no doubt, but with clearly explicit references to the emperor
and patriarch in Constantinople[13]. By the first decade of the ninth

---

[11] Constantin Bacha, *Les oeuvres arabes de Théodore Aboucara, évêque de Haran*
(Beyrouth, 1904), pp. 60-61. That Abū Qurrah would have composed this work
in Syriac need cause no surprise, because in the oriental patriarchates, Syriac was
the preferred language of theological discourse among the 'Jacobites' with whom
he was in controversy on the subject of the theological understanding of Christ's
death.

[12] See H. Kennedy, *The Early Abbasid Caliphate: a Political History* (London,
1981); J. Lassner, *The Shaping of ʿAbbasid Rule* (Princeton, 1980); D. Sourdel, *Le
vizirat abbaside* (2 vols.; Damascus, 1959-1960).

[13] See B. Kotter (ed.), *Die Schriften des Johannes von Damaskos*. Vol. III, *Contra Imaginum Calumniatores Orationes Tres* (Berlin & New York, 1975).

century, after fifty years of Abbasid rule, when the icons were again a focus of controversy for Christians in the caliphate, Theodore Abū Qurrah responded with an Arabic tract in defense of the veneration of the icons. He addressed it to an official of the church of the Icon of Christ in Edessa, with reference to the Jews and Muslims of the caliphate. There is no reference at all to Byzantium or to the Second Council of Nicea which had been held in the year 787 specifically to condemn iconoclasm[14].

From what Abū Qurrah wrote it is clear that the icon problem which the 'Melkites' faced in the caliphate had to do with the public veneration of the symbols of Christianity in an Islamic environment in which the caliph's policies since the time of ʿAbd al-Malik (685-705) had been to claim the public space for Islam[15]. Moreover, the icons and the cross actually proclaimed what the *Qur'ān* denies in regard to Jesus, son of Mary, and his mother[16]. By the first decade of the ninth century, when Abū Qurrah wrote his treatise, there was already a second generation of Christians who refused to perform the public veneration of the icons for fear of the reproach of "anti-Christians, especially ones claiming to have in hand a scripture sent down from God,…imputing to them the worship of idols, and the transgression of what God commanded in the Torah and the Prophets." Among Christian leaders of the time, there is really no evidence in Syria/Palestine of a Byzantine iconoclastic attitude, but there do seem to have been

[14] See G. Dumeige, *Nicée II* (Histoire des Conciles Oecuméniques, vol. 4; Paris, 1978); F. Boespflug et N. Lossky (eds.), *Nicée II, 787-1987; douze siècles d'images religieuses* (Paris, 1987).

[15] See S. H. Griffith, "Images, Islam and Christian Icons," in Pierre Canivet & Jean-Paul Rey-Coquais (eds.), *La Syrie, de Byzance à l'Islam, VIIe-VIIIe siècles* (Damas, 1992), pp. 121-138.

[16] See G. R. D. King, "Islam, Iconoclasm, and the Declaration of Doctrine," *Bulletin of the School of Oriental and African Studies* 48 (1985), pp. 267-277.

disagreements over church policy about what stance to take in the face of a strong Islamic reaction to the public veneration of icons. Some leaders may well have been in favor of down-playing the traditional devotions for the sake of peace. After all, in the world of Islam, unlike that of Byzantium, both cross and icon go together as the public symbols which elicit the roproaches of Muslims and Jews. And the most likely explanation for the defacement of the figures of living beings in Christian churches in the late eighth century in Palestine and Transjordan is that Muslims sometimes worshipped in Christian churches at the time[17], and this circumstance went a long way toward explaining the rise of local Christian iconophobia, rather than a specific concern for the policies of the synod of Hiereia (754)[18].

There are only two dates assigned to events in Abū Qurrah's life which survive in the available historical documentation to guide the would-be biographer. Both of them appear in Syriac chronicles by Syrian Orthodox, or 'Jacobite' writers: the chronicle of Michael the Syrian and the anonymous chronicle ad annum 1234, composed by a now unknown writer from Edessa around the year 1240. Michael the Syrian reports as follows:

> In the year 1125 (i.e. 813-814 A.D.), a Chalcedonian of Edessa named Theodoricus and surnamed Pygla, who for a short time had been bishop of Ḥarrān and who had been deposed by their patriarch

[17] See Suliman Bashear, "Qibla Musharriqa and Early Muslim Prayer in Churches," *The Muslim World* 81 (1991), pp. 267-282.

[18] *Pace* M.-F. Auzépy, "De la Palestine à Constantinople (VIIIe-IXe siècles): Étienne le Sabaïte et Jean Damascène," *Travaux et Mémoires* 12 (1994), pp. 183-218, see p. 193, n. 77. On the whole issue of the mosaic pavements, their defacement, and their subsequent repair in the eighth century, see the full discussion in the forthcoming book of Robert Schick, *The Christian Communities of Palestine from Byzantine to Islamic Rule; a Historical and Archaeological Study* (Princeton, 1996).

Theodoret because of charges brought against him, betook himself
about the countries perverting the conscience of Chalcedonian and
Orthodox persons. He propagated the doctrine of Maximus and
even added to the impiety of that man. ... He went to Alexandria,
and because he was a sophist and entered into disputes by his arguments against the pagans (i.e., *ḥanpê*, the Muslims), as he knew the
Saracen language, he aroused the admiration of the simple people.
But since he did not succeed at Alexandria, he departed for Armenia.
He arrived in the presence of the *patricios* Ashot, and from the first
meeting he seduced him and rendered him favorable. ... Then patriarch Cyriacus sent Nonnus, the archdeacon of Nisibis, to unmask
his heretical ideas so that he would not deceive the Armenians. ...
Nonnus delivered Ashot from both Dyophysitism and Julianism[19].

Michael the Syrian pinpoints the year 813/814 as the one in
which Theodore Abū Qurrah[20] began a journey which took him
from Alexandria in Egypt to Armenia, on what amounts to a pilgrimage of religious controversy, in an effort to win adherents
from the 'Monophysite' community to the Dyophysite views of
the followers of St. Maximus the Confessor. It informs us that earlier Abū Qurrah had been deposed as bishop of Ḥarrān by the
Melkite patriarch of Antioch, Theodoret, who is now believed to
have reigned before 787, and probably from around 785 to 799[21].

[19] J.-B. Chabot, *Chronique de Michel le Syrien; patriarche jacobite d'Antioche* (4 vols.; Paris, 1899-1910), vol. III, pp. 32-34 (French), vol. IV, p. 496 (Syriac).

[20] One will not readily miss the demeaning intention behind Michael the Syrian's name for Abū Qurrah, "Theodoricus Pygla". He uses the diminutive form of 'Theodore', coupled with the Syriac word for 'radish', which is probably a reference to the Arabic word '*qurrah*', which also has a vegetal sense, being the word for 'water cress'. One scholar has suggested that a colloquial pronunciation of the words 'Abū Qurrah' as something like "bû gra," might have prompted the adoption of the derogatory name 'Pygla'. See Mechtild Kellerman-Rost, "Ein pseudo-aristotelischer Traktat über die Tugend," (Unpublished Ph.D. dissertation; Erlangen, 1965), p. 21.

[21] See V. Grumel, *La Chronologie* (Paris, 1958), p. 447 and J. Nasrallah, *Histoire du mouvement littéraire*, pp. 16 & 112. Nasrallah has argued convincingly

In Armenia Abū Qurrah is said to have appeared in the court of a prince named Ashot, who chronologically must have been the Bagratid Armenian prince Ashot Msaker, who died in the year 826[22]. The Syrian Orthodox patriarch Cyriacus, who is said to have sent the deacon Nonnus of Nisibis to Armenia to debate Abū Qurrah, reigned from 793 to 817, thereby providing a *terminus ante quem* for Abū Qurrah's appearance in the presence of Ashot, i.e., before the year 817[23]. According to Michael the Syrian therefore, Abū Qurrah was briefly the bishop of Ḥarrān until some point before 785 and 799, and he was an itinerant controversialist in the Chalcedonian cause for four years or so, from 813 to 817, culminating in the Armenian venture.

The reported debate in Armenia, which is confirmed by references in the Arabic works of the Jacobite apologist Ḥabīb ibn Ḥidmah Abū Rā'iṭah, a contemporary of Abū Qurrah's[24], calls to mind the "Letter to the Armenians," which patriarch Thomas of Jerusalem (807-821) issued to "those practicing heresy in Armenia[25]". Theodore Abū Qurrah wrote the letter for Patriarch Thomas in Arabic, and Michael Synkellos translated it into Greek and dispatched it, according to the letter's superscription. Michael became *synkellos* in Jerusalem in 811 and went off to Constantinople at the

that Job was patriarch in Antioch from 799 to 843. See his "Regard critique sur I. Dick, *Th. Abū Qurrah, De l'existence du Créateur et de la vraie religion*," *Proche Orient Chrétien* 36 (1986), pp. 46-62; 37 (1987), pp. 63-70, esp. vol. 36, pp. 61-62.

[22] See I. Dick, "Un continuateur arabe," p. 116; A. Van Roey, *Nonnus de Nisibe, traité apologétique, étude, texte et traduction* (Bibliothèque du Muséon, vol. 21; Louvain, 1948), p. 18.

[23] Actually, it was Abū Rā'iṭah who sent Nonnus. See Van Roey, *Nonnus de Nisibe*, p. 18. For patriarch Cyriacus' dates see Grumel, *La Chronologie*, p. 449.

[24] See Georg Graf, *Die Schriften des Jacobiten Ḥabīb ibn Ḥidma Abū Rā'iṭa* (CSCO, vols. 130 & 131; Louvain, 1951), vol. 130, pp. 65-66, 73, 75-76, 79-80, 82-83.

[25] *PG*, vol. 97, cols. 1504-1521.

patriarch's behest, never to return, around 815. He spent several
years, c.811 to 813 in Edessa[26], leaving the year 814 as the probable
year in which the letter was written and translated, and thereby
suggesting Abū Qurrah's presence in the holy city in the same
year, the year in which he began the journey which Michael the
Syrian reports, and which eventually brought him to Armenia,
perhaps carrying Patriarch Thomas' letter.

The anonymous Syriac chronicle *ad annum* 1234 reports another
event in Abū Qurrah's life, in which he appears as an apologist for
Christianity in the Islamic milieu, and specifically in a conversation
with the caliph al-Ma'mūn (813-833). According to the report,

> In the year 1140 of the Greeks, 214 of the Ṭayyāyê,... Ma'mūn came
> to reach Ḥarrān. Theodore, the bishop of Ḥarrān, who was named
> Abū Qurrah, got into a conversation with Ma'mūn. There was a
> great debate between them about the faith of the Christians. The
> debate is written in a special book for anyone who wants to read it[27].

The year of this reported conversation was 829 A.D[28]. The loca-
tion in Ḥarrān suggests that by this time, which must have been
toward the end of his life, Abū Qurrah had regained the bishopric
from which he had been ejected at some point between 785 and
799, according to Michael the Syrian, when Theodoret was the
Melkite patriarch of Antioch.

Taken together the two chronicle reports of Theodore Abū
Qurrah and his activities, and what can be deduced from them,

---

[26] See "Michael Synkellos" in A. P. Kazhdan & A.-M. Talbot et al. (eds.), *The Oxford Dictionary of Byzantium* (3 vols.; New York, 1991), vol. 2, pp. 1369-1370.

[27] J.-B. Chabot, *Anonymi Auctoris Chronicon ad A.C. 1234 Pertinens* (CSCO, vols. 81, 82, 109, 354; Louvain; 1916, 1920, 1937 & 1974), vol. 109, pp. 22-23. The name 'Theodore' is clearly in the text, not "Theodosius", as in the translation in vol. 354, p. 16.

[28] According to the tables in Grumel, *La Chronologie*, p. 250.

provide a chronological framework for his biography which stretches from a point within the last fifteen years of the eighth century, when for a time he was bishop of Ḥarrān, through the years 813 to 817, when he was on an apologetical pilgrimage from Jerusalem to Alexandria, and on to Armenia, and finally reaching the year 829 when he was again a resident bishop in Ḥarrān. Whatever else can be learned about Abū Qurrah's life must then take these approximately forty years between 785 and 829 as his *floruit*.

With these dates in place, i.e., the forty years between 785 and 829 as Abū Qurrah's *floruit*, one may then attempt by inference and extrapolation to sketch an outline of his life. In all probability he was born in Edessa. The evidence for this supposition is twofold. Michael the Syrian called him "an Edessan Chalcedonian[29]". And in his own Arabic treatise on the veneration of the holy icons Abū Qurrah made a special mention of Edessa's famous icon of Christ, saying, "Of all the icons, we mention it here because it is honored with veneration in our own city, Edessa the Blest." The fact that on his own testimony Abū Qurrah also wrote in Syriac[30], supports his Syrian origins, and Edessa, of course, was in his day the metropolis *par excellence* for the speakers of Syriac.

The year of Abū Qurrah's birth can only be conjectured. One must postulate a date early enough to allow him to have achieved an age at which he could plausibly have been consecrated bishop of Ḥarrān and have held the office until he was deposed by Patriarch Theodoret between 785 and 799. At the same time, the date of his birth must be late enough for him not to have been impossibly old at the time of his conversation with the caliph al-Ma'mūn in the year 829. Within these constraints one might reasonably conjecture

[29] Chabot, *Chronique de Michel le Syrien*, vol. III, p. 32; vol. IV, p. 495.
[30] Bacha, *Les oeuvres arabes*, pp. 60-61.

that Abū Qurrah was born around the year 755, making him about thirty years of age in 785 and seventy-four years old in 829[31].

Before Abū Qurrah became the bishop of Ḥarrān, an office it is not unreasonable to assume that he regained after Patriarch Theodoret's death in 799, given the fact that the chronicle *ad annum* 1234 calls him "bishop of Ḥarrān" in 829, he was in all likelihood a monk of the monastery of Mar Sabas in the Judean desert.

Abū Qurrah's association with Mar Sabas has long been assumed by scholars on the basis of his manifest intellectual debt to St. John of Damascus, the monastery's most illustrious theological scholar, a debt most evident in Abū Qurrah's tract on the veneration of the icons.. The debt is acknowledged in the transmission of one of the Greek works ascribed to Abū Qurrah by the phrase *diá phônēs Iôánnou Damaskēnou* which appears at the head of his Greek *opusculum* 18[32]. The phrase need mean no more than that Abū Qurrah here presents what amounts to St. John's teaching on the subject at hand, the refutation of Muslims[33]. But on a broader theological horizon, in Syrian circles Abū Qurrah's name is also associated with that of John of Damascus. Bar Hebraeus,

---

[31] Both Khalil Samir and the present writer have independently arrived at the year 755 as a reasonable suggestion for Abū Qurrah's year of birth. See Kh. Samir, "La 'somme des aspects de la foi,' oeuvre de Abū Qurrah?" *Orientalia Christiana Analecta* 226 (1986) pp. 119-120. Both of us think the earlier dates suggested by Graf (740, in *Die arabischen Schriften*, p. 20) and Nasrallah (724/725, in *Histoire du mouvement littéraire*, vol. II, tome 2, p. 110) are implausibly early, based as they are on what seems to be the unwarranted assumption that Abū Qurrah met St. John of Damascus in his lifetime. Ignace Dick suggested the year 750 (in "Un continuateur arabe," p. 120), but he reckoned without the testimony of the chronicle *ad annum* 1234 to the effect that Abū Qurrah encountered the caliph al-Ma'mūn in the year 829.

[32] *PG*, 94, col. 1596.

[33] See Marcel Richard, "*Apo Phonês*," *Byzantion* 20 (1950), pp. 191-222.

for example, remarks at one point that "the Greeks had always confessed one will and one operation in Christ, until the time of Maximus, Theodoric [*sic*] of Ḥarrān, and John of Damascus[34]". The point is that the sources themselves associate Abū Qurrah's teaching with that of John of Damascus. But none of this requires that Abū Qurrah have been at Mar Sabas in John of Damascus' lifetime. The works of Mar Sabas' most famous Greek-writing monk would have been available to transmit his thought to those who came after him. And in Abū Qurrah's treatise on the icons his borrowings from John of Damascus have a decidedly documentary character, as a quick glance at the text will show.

A document which explicitly ties Theodore Abū Qurrah to Mar Sabas monastery is the tenth-century Georgian version of the passion of St. Michael, a monk of the monastery[35]. In the judgment of Paulus Peeters the account of the monk Michael's encounter with the caliph ᶜAbd al-Malik, his defence of the Christian faith and his polemic against Islam, followed by his execution, was first composed in Arabic in Abbasid times, perhaps in the ninth century, and only later translated into Georgian[36]. A certain Basil, a priest of St. Sabas, is the reputed narrator of the passion story, the same Basil who, as Basil of Emesa, is later credited with the composition

[34] Joseph S. Assemanus, *Bibliotheca Orientalis* (Rome, 1721), vol. II, p. 292, n. 3.

[35] On the manuscript and its date see R. P. Blake, "Catalogue des manuscrits géorgiens de la bibliothèque de la laure d'Iviron au mont Athos," *Revue de l'Orient Chrétien* 23, 3rd. ser., 8 (1931-1932), pp. 324-325. A new study of this document, along with an English translation of the Georgian text is forthcoming in *ARAM* vol. 6 [1997]: S. H. Griffith, "Michael, the Martyr and Monk of Mar Sabas Monastery, at the Court of the Caliph ᶜAbd al-Malik; Christian Apologetics and Martyrology in the Early Islamic Period," and Monica J. Blanchard, "The Georgian Version of the Martyrdom of Saint Michael, Monk of Mar Sabas Monastery."

[36] See P. Peeters, "La passion de s. Michel le Sabaïte," *Analecta Bollandiana* 48 (1930), pp. 65, 77, 80.

of the life of St. Theodore of Edessa[37], which in the judgment of
Paulus Peeters is a piece of hagiographical fiction based on the life
of Theodore Abū Qurrah[38]! The passion of St. Michael is repeated,
with variations, in the life of Theodore of Edessa. The narrator
Basil claims that he heard the story of St. Michael at Mar Sabas
monastery from "Abū Qurrah, the neophyte of Saint Sabas, the
pastor and hierarch of Assyria, and the wonder-worker of Babylon[39]". Basil claims to have gone to Theodore Abū Qurrah's cell,
"at the side of the laura, in the cleft ravine on the way to the Jordan and the Dead Sea," where "Abū Qurrah told us the story[40]".

While the Passion of St. Michael comes from after the time of
Abū Qurrah, and presumes his fame, it nevertheless is arguably a
testimony from a ninth-century Christian Arabic source which
identifies him as a monk of Mar Sabas. The fact that the text
depicts Abū Qurrah as a mature monastic father with disciples,
and closes with an encomium of St. Sabas as, "a spiritual leader,
possessed of such disciples as Stephen, John, Thomas, and
Theodore Abū Qurrah[41]", does not require the reader to conclude
that Abū Qurrah was an old man when Basil met him at Mar
Sabas monastery. Rather, in Basil's account, written after Abū
Qurrah's lifetime, the latter's fame has colored the narrative considerably. And it may be taken simply as a testimony that Abū
Qurrah was for some time a monk of Mar Sabas. One may then
reasonably suppose that the first period of his monastic life was in
all probability prior to his episcopal consecration as the bishop of
Ḥarrān.

[37] See A. Vasiliev, "The Life of St. Theodore of Edessa," *Byzantion* 16 (1944),
pp. 165-225.
[38] See P. Peeters, "La passion de s. Michel," pp. 89-91.
[39] Peeters, "La passion de s. Michel," p. 77.
[40] Peeters, "La passion de s. Michel," pp. 66-67.
[41] Peeters, "La passion de s. Michel," p. 76.

Finally, as an oblique testimony to Abū Qurrah's association with Mar Sabas monastery one might cite the fact that the copying of his Arabic works was an accomplishment credited to that monastery. At the end of his letter to the 'Jacobite' David, for example, one finds the commendation of the reader to "the prayers of our holy father Saba, in whose monastery the text was copied from which this text was copied[42]".

Theodore Abū Qurrah has been identified by some scholars, following the suggestion of Paul Kraus, with the "Theodore" (*Thayādurus*) whom both Ibn an-Nadīm and al-Qiftī named as the first translator of Aristotle's *Analytica Priora* into Arabic[43]. Richard Walzer called Kraus' suggestion a "convincing guess," noting that Abū Qurrah's master, St. John of Damascus, was known for his interest in Aristotle's logic, to the exclusion of the *Analytica Posteriora*[44]. Others have been more hesitant to endorse the suggestion, saying the 'Theodore' in question simply cannot now be identified[45], or that 'perhaps' he was Abū Qurrah[46], or that the fact of the matter "is not altogether clear[47]". However, one might point out that it was not merely the coincidence of the name 'Theodore' which prompted it, but the fact that in his *Kitāb al-Ḥayawān* al-Jāḥiẓ (d. 868 A.D.) seems to have named Abū

[42] Bacha, *Les oeuvres arabes*, p. 139.

[43] P. Kraus, "Zu Ibn al-Muqaffaᶜ," *Rivista degli Studi Orientali* 14 (1933), p. 3, n. 3.

[44] R. Walzer, "New Light on the Arabic Translation of Aristotle," in *Greek into Arabic; Essays on Islamic Philosophy* (Oriental Studies, 1; Oxford, 1962), p. 68.

[45] So N. Rescher, *Al-Farabi's Short Commentary on Aristotle's Prior Analytics* (Pittsburgh, 1963), p. 32.

[46] So Bayard Dodge, *The Fihrist of al-Nadīm* (New York, 1970), vol. II, p. IIII.

[47] So D. M. Dunlop, *Arab Civilization to A.D. 1500* (London, 1971), p. 316. n. 21.

Qurrah in a list of the translators of Aristotle known to him[48]. Unfortunately, the list is not without its problems. Specifically, the name of Abū Qurrah, which appears in two places in the work of al-Jāḥiẓ just cited, may be a mistake in the manuscript transmission of the *Kitāb al Ḥayawān* for the name of Thābit ibn Qurrah (836-901), a well known translator of Greek texts, who was also a native of Ḥarrān[49]. So the identification of Abū Qurrah, the bishop of Ḥarrān, with the Theodore who first translated the *Analytica Priora* into Arabic must remain tentative. One might enlist the precedent of Abū Qurrah's better attested translation of what was thought to be Aristotle's *De virtutibus animae* for Ṭahir ibn al-Ḥusayn. But whatever might be one's judgment in the matter, there can be no doubt about Abū Qurrah's competence to do the translation, or about his interest in the subject matter, as his surviving works amply testify. He was a scholar bishop, who was fluent in Arabic and who had a taste for religious controversy of the very sort which prompted both Muslims and Christians in his day to an interest in Aristotelian logic.

Throughout his career, Abū Qurrah's principal claim to fame was his skill as an apologist for Chalcedonian Christianity in the Arabic language. He was a controversialist, a *mutakallim*, who not only argued on behalf of his Melkite faith, but who went to some trouble to elaborate a conceptual framework in Arabic, in terms of which he hoped to commend the veracity of his confessional position to others, particularly to members of other Christian denominations, those whom he called 'Jacobites' and 'Nestorians', as well

---

[48] See ʿAmr ibn Baḥr al-Jāḥiẓ, *Kitāb al-Ḥayawān* (Cairo, 1938), vol. I, pp. 75-79. See a French translation of the important passages in Abdurrahman Badawi, *La transmission de la philosophie grecque au monde arabe* (Etudes de Philosophie Médiévale, 56; Paris, 1968), pp. 21-24.

[49] See J. Ruska, "Thābit b. Kurra," *EI*, vol. IV, pp. 770-771.

as to the Muslims. And there are a number of testimonies preserved in the sources to testify to Abū Qurrah's reputation in this regard.

Ḥabīb ibn Ḥidmah Abū Rā'iṭah, a Syrian Orthodox contemporary and antagonist of Abū Qurrah, in his complaints about him, preserves a record of Abū Qurrah as a controversialist. Abū Rā'iṭah calls him a 'scholar' or a 'savant' (ʿālim), a 'sage' (ḥakīm), and a 'philosopher' (al-faylasūf)[50]. He also qualifies him as a "Melkite, Chalcedonian, Maximist" who uses tricks "against simple, negligent believers, so that they will not think he is a Nestorian[51]".

Among the Muslims too the memory of Abū Qurrah as a controversialist was recorded. There is, for example, an entry in the *Fihrist* of Ibn an-Nadīm which reads as follows:

> There was also Abū Qurrah. He was the Melkite bishop of Ḥarrān. Among his books there is one in which he attacks Nestorius, the leader. A group has in turn denounced him for it[52].

However, for our purposes it is particularly interesting to note that the composite annals of Christian history which the Melkite community preserved under the name of Eutychius of Alexandria contain the memory of Abū Qurrah's participation in the controversy over the veneration of icons, and note that "he wrote a

---

[50] See Graf, *Die Schriften des Abū Rā'iṭa*, vol. 130, pp. 65-66, 73, 79, 86.

[51] Graf, *Die Schriften des Abū Rā'iṭa*, vol. 130, p. 68.

[52] Gustav Flügel, *Kitāb al-Fihrist* (New photo-ed.; Beirut, 1964), p. 24. The reading adopted here was first proposed by I. Krackovskij, "Theodore Abū Kurra in the Muslim Writers of the Ninth-Tenth Centuries," [Russian] *Christianskij Vostok* 4 (1915), p. 306. For a fuller study of Abū Qurrah as controversialist, and the various Christian and Muslim testimonies in this regard, see Sidney H. Griffith, *Theodore Abū Qurrah: the Intellectual Profile of an Arab Christian Writer of the First Abbasid Century* (The Tel Aviv University Irene Halmos Chair of Arabic Literature Annual Lecture; Tel Aviv, 1992).

book about it and called it, 'The Treatise on the Veneration of Images'⁵³".

There is one potentially pertinent item to mention in connection with Abū Qurrah's biography. It is a speculative point, concerning the reason for his demotion from the see of Ḥarrān by the demand of Patriarch Theodoret between 785 and 799. Michael the Syrian says merely, "When he was a bishop in Ḥarrān a short time, because of an indictment which was brought against him, he was deposed by Theodoret, their patriarch⁵⁴".

Neither Michael's sources, nor any other early document specifies the nature of the indictment brought against Abū Qurrah so soon after his installation in Ḥarrān. Among modern scholars, Ignace Dick opines that like the famous Jacob of Edessa a century earlier, Abū Qurrah may have resigned his see out of frustration with his patriarch and to devote himself to scholarship and inter-religious controversy⁵⁵. Dick notes in this connection that in spite of his trouble with Patriarch Theodoret of Antioch, Abū Qurrah was always in good repute in Jerusalem. Jerusalem was not only the stalwart champion of Christological orthodoxy; she was also the see from whose ranks came some of the most notable apologists for the icons in the eighth and ninth centuries, from John of Damascus to Theodore Abū Qurrah himself, not to mention such others as the brothers Graptoi, Michael Synkellos, Theophane the Chronicler, and a whole host of persons with connections in the Studite monastery in Constantinople⁵⁶.

---

⁵³ L. Cheikho, et al. (eds.), *Eutychii Patriarchae Alexandrini Annales* (CSCO, vol. 51; Beirut, 1909), p. 64.
⁵⁴ Chabot, *Chronique de Michel le Syrien,* vol. III, p. 332 (French); vol. IV, p. 495 (Syriac).
⁵⁵ See Dick, "Un continuateur arabe," p. 124.
⁵⁶ On the Studite monastery and the iconoclast controversy see Paul Alexander, *The Patriarch Nicephorus of Constantinople; Ecclesiastical Policy and Image*

Perhaps it will not strain credibility to the breaking point to suggest that it could have been his position in favor of the public veneration of the icons that put Abū Qurrah on a collision course with Patriarch Theodoret of Antioch. There were those in the Christian communities in the caliphate in Abū Qurrah's day and earlier, who, as he said in his treatise on the veneration of the icons, were abandoning the practice of venerating them because of the reproach of others, Jews and Muslims, who accused them of idolatry. While there is no mention in Abū Qurrah's work of hierarchs among these misguided Christians, it is not difficult to imagine in those times, that even a patriarch could have courted peace with the Muslim authorities by requiring his followers to lower the public profile of Christian devotional display. After all, it is clear from both Islamic and Christian sources that in the eighth and early ninth centuries, the issue of the veneration of the cross and the icons was an instance of contention between Muslims and Christians in the caliphate[57]. In point of fact, Abū Qurrah's troubles were with Patriarch Theodoret (c.785-799). It is noticeable that in the surviving evidence, both Theodoret's predecessor in office, Patriarch Theodore in 763, and his successor, Patriarch Job in 836, are each said to have publicly affirmed their iconophile faith, in concert with the patriarchs of Alexandria and Jerusalem[58]. As for

Worship in the Byzantine Empire (Oxford, 1958); Stephen Gero, *Byzantine Iconoclasm during the Reign of Constantine V* (*C*SCO, vol. 384, Louvain, 1977).

[57] See Sidney H. Griffith, "Images, Islam and Christian Icons; a Moment in the Christian/Muslim Encounter in Early Islamic Times," pp. 121-138.

[58] For the 763 synod in Jerusalem see Mansi, vol. XII, col. 680. On the 836 synod and its alleged letter to the Byzantine emperor, see the text of the letter in L. Duchesne, "L'iconographie byzantine dans un document grec du IXe siècle," *Roma e l'Oriente* 5 (1912-1913), pp. 222-239, 273-285, 349-366. There are problems about the authenticity of the letter. See I. Ševčenko, "Constantinople Viewed from the Eastern Provinces in the Middle Byzantine Period," *Harvard Ukrainian Studies* 3-4 (1979-1980), p. 735, n. 36.

Patriarch Theodoret, there is evidence of a local synod in Antioch during his reign, in that Theodore Studites quoted a passage from its acts in one of his letters to John the Grammarian. The passage, naturally, favors the veneration of the icons, and it concludes with the statement that "we venerate Christ himself, and not the artfully figured material in the icon"[59] — a point worthy of Abū Qurrah himself. It is evidence, albeit slim, that the veneration of the holy icons was an issue of controversy in Theodoret's reign, and it is notable that the endorsement of the iconophile position is laconic in the extreme.

Abū Qurrah was presumably installed as bishop of Ḥarrān by Patriarch Theodore of Antioch toward the end of his reign, around the year 785. Having been deposed by Patriarch Theodoret, Abū Qurrah presumably regained his see with the accession of Patriarch Job to the throne of Antioch in 799. Job was an iconophile, and a translator of the works of Aristotle into Arabic[60]; it is not surprising that Abū Qurrah's career flourished under his patriarchate. The question is: is it at all plausible that the controversy over the icons could have estranged Abū Qurrah's from Patriarch Theodoret? In favor of the hypothesis one might point out that no other theological issue is likely to have been the cause of the crisis, given Abū Qurrah's staunch orthodoxy. Other than a problem over the veneration of the icons, which was the only real question of the day between fellow Melkites, some disciplinary matter could conceivably have been the issue between Abū Qurrah and the Patriarch. But in that case one would expect that particularly Abū Qurrah's Syrian Orthodox adversaries would have recorded it. Whereas to accuse him of having defended the icons would scarcely blacken his name among them.

---

[59] *PG*, vol. 99, col. 1592.

[60] See Nasrallah, *Histoire du mouvement littéraire*, vol. II, tome 2, pp. 34-55.

The Composition of the Treatise

Abū Qurrah wrote his Arabic treatise on the veneration of the holy icons after the year 799. This year is the likely *terminus post quem* for the composition because in it he mentions the martyrdom of Anthony Rawḥ, which took place on 25 December 799[61]. At some point in 813/814, Abū Qurrah became involved with Patriarch Thomas of Jerusalem's campaign to promote the faith of Chalcedon among the Armenians, and thereby began the Christological phase of his apologetic career[62]. Consequently, it makes good sense to suppose that he wrote his tract on the icons in the first decade of the ninth century, when he regained his episcopal see in Ḥarrān, under the notably iconophile Patriarch Job. At some point during this period Abū Qurrah wrote a tract in which he defended the thesis that "making prostration to the icon of Christ, our God, who became incarnate from the Holy Spirit, and from the pure Virgin Mary, as well as to the icons of the saints, is incumbent upon every Christian."

The circumstance which elicited Abū Qurrah's treatise was a situation which manifested itself at the Church of the Icon of Christ in the metropolitan city of Edessa, to whose archbishopric Ḥarrān was a suffragan see. The problem was, as Abū Qurrah put it, that "many Christians are abandoning prostration to the icon of Christ our God," because "anti-Christians... are reprimanding them for their prostration... and they sneer at them." Moreover, Abū Qurrah suggests that in the instance of the holy icon of

---

[61] See Dick, *Icônes*, p. 173. Ignace Dick, "La passion arabe de s. Antoine Ruwaḥ, néomartyr de Damas (†25 déc. 799)," *Le Muséon* 74 (1961), pp. 109-133; and Khalil Samir, "Saint Rawḥ al-Qurašī. Étude d'onomastique arabe et authenticité de sa passion," *Le Muséon* 105 (1992), pp. 343-359.

[62] See Griffith, "Reflections on the Biography of Theodore Abū Qurrah," pp. 163-164.

Edessa, by the time he wrote his tract the pastoral problem of some Christians refusing to venerate it was already a generation old, a circumstance which further suggests that the matter was an issue already in the time of Patriarch Theodoret and even before.

Abū Qurrah addressed the treatise to "Abba Yannah, our brother, you are here with us in Edessa." Ignace Dick has proposed that the form of address supposes that Yannah is a brother bishop to Abū Qurrah. He suggests that it was John (Yannah being a form of the name Yuḥannā), the bishop of Edessa, whom Dick wants to identify with the John of Edessa of whom we have manuscript reports of his having participated in public debates about religion in the presence of Caliph Harūn ar-Rašīd (786-809)[63].

While the chronology favors this identification, the form of the name Yannah draws one's attention to the fact that in the colophon of a Syriac manuscript written under Melkite auspices in Edessa in 723 A.D., there twice appears the name Y-n-y (Yannay, Yannī/Yannā) attributed to both the *higoumenos* and the priest and *chartularius* respectively of the "house of the image of the Lord: in Edessa[64]. It is clear that the name Yannah in Arabic is a form of the name John, but it is interesting to note that in the Melkite colophon of Edessa the name John in its customary form Yuḥannan appears right after the two occurences of the name Y-n-y[65]. This fact suggests that while the two forms may be etymologically related, they may in fact be used to identify different people. Here it suggests that Abū Qurrah addressed his Arabic tract on the veneration of the holy icons not to John the bishop of

[63] See Dick, *Icônes,* p. 39 (Arabic introduction). On John of Edessa see *GCAL*, II, p. 25.

[64] The colophon is published in R. W. Thomson, "An Eighth-Century Melkite Colophon from Edessa," *Journal of Theological Studies* 13 (1962), p. 253.

[65] See Khalil Samir, "Yannah dans l'onomastique arabo-copte," in *Orientalia Christiana Periodica* 45 (1979), pp. 166-170.

Edessa, but to Yannah, an official at the Church of the Icon of Christ which was the focus of Abū Qurrah's comments in his treatise.

The circumstances of Abū Qurrah's treatise on the icons indicate that there was in his day and place a major pastoral problem in connection with the veneration of icons, and that Abū Qurrah himself was heavily involved with the controversy. On a more personal note, the timing of his treatise, coming immediately after his presumed restoration as bishop of Ḥarrān has the ring of one vindicated about it, at the same time it marks an important point in Abū Qurrah's career as a Melkite apologist.

When all is said and done, we know little about the life of the first Christian apologist whose name we know, who wrote regularly in Arabic. Much of what we do know must be inferred from passages in the works of others, allusions in his own works, and remarks by the scribes who copied the manuscripts in which his works survive. The works themselves are the surest route to knowledge of him. And they stand as the first systematic attempt clearly to state the basic teachings of the Christian faith in the Arabic idiom of the *Qur'ān*.

The Argument of the Treatise on the Veneration of the Holy Icons

Doctrinally, Theodore Abū Qurrah was a student of John Damascene. In his treatise on image veneration, as indeed in all of his works, there is no appreciable progression of ideas beyond what his master had achieved. Abū Qurrah's originality consists in the genius with which he expressed John's arguments in Arabic. On every page of this treatise, one finds the arguments of the earlier scholars deployed to meet the needs of the new generation of Christians, who spoke Arabic, and who were more evidently in debate with Muslims than were their parents. References to Muslims and to their ideas, allusions to the *Qur'ān* and to the Islamic tradition are the novelties in Abū Qurrah's treatise, from the point of view of its intellectual content[66].

It is clear that in the twenty-four chapters of the treatise Abū Qurrah was concerned to reinforce the conviction of his Christian readers of the rectitude of their habitual practice of venerating images. He also intended to furnish them with ready replies with which they might defend themselves against the charge that the veneration of images is no more than idolatry. Furthermore, following John of Damascus, he argued that any Christian who would give up the veneration of images, for fear of being accused of idolatry, must logically give up all forms of the public exercise of his religion.

Abū Qurrah presented his arguments in five broad strokes. First, he argued that it is not a valid contention against images to allege that they imply the attribution of bodiliness to God. All scriptural language, be it in the Old Testament, the Gospel, or the *Qur'ān*, speaks of God in terms that of themselves imply bodiliness, because human knowledge proceeds necessarily from the sensible to the intelligible. Images are the writing of the illiterate. Therefore, the bodiliness which images imply is no more attributable to God than is the bodiliness which the language of the scriptures implies.

Secondly, even though the veneration of images is not enjoined on Christians in the Bible, Abū Qurrah argues that the practice

---

[66] More information about this treatise on the veneration of icons can be found in Sidney H. Griffith, "Theodore Abū Qurrah's Arabic Tract on the Christian Practice of Venerating Images," *Journal of the American Oriental Society* 105 (1984), pp. 53-73; idem, "Theodore Abū Qurrah's On the Veneration of the Holy Icons," *The Sacred Art Journal* 13 (1992), pp. 3-19.

must be apostolic in origin, because images are found in all of the churches of every country. To reject them because there is no mention of them in the New Testament would require one logically to reject other things not mentoned there, concerning the apostolic foundations of which no one has a doubt — e.g., the eucharistic formulae and various other liturgical practices.

In the third place, Abū Qurrah cites passages from three of the fathers, the "teachers" of the church, as he calls them, which, he says, attest to the early presence of images in the church, and to the legitimacy of venerating them. He cites passages from the pseudo-Athanasian *Quaestiones ad Antiochum Ducem*, which both Abū Qurrah and John of Damascus took to be authentic; from Eusebius of Caesarea's report in the *Ecclesiastical History* about the image of Christ at Baniyas, erected by the woman whom Christ had cured of the issue of blood; a story from the "fathers of Jerusalem" about an image of Mary which allayed a monk's temptations; and finally some sentences from Gregory the Theologian about the venerability of Christ's cradle and the stone on which he was laid in Bethlehem. The argument here is simply that anyone who would depart from the practice (*aš-šarīʿah*) of these Christian teachers, has in effect departed from Christianity[67].

By far the longest set of arguments in the treatise is the one which comprises the fourth step, in which Abū Qurrah spends ten of his twenty-four chapters explaining how the Christian habit of venerating images does not come under the ban against idols which is recorded in Exodus 20:2-5 and in Deuteronomy 6:13 (10:20).

---

[67] Abū Qurrah's argument from the fathers is presented in chapter 8. All of these stories are also to be found in John of Damascus' discourses, with the exception of the one from Gregory the Theologian. See Kotter, *Contra Imaginum Calumniatores Orationes Tres*, pp. 124, 169, 173, 191. The use of the term *aš-šarīʿah* reflects the Islamic ambience.

There is nothing new in the argument, which goes beyond what John of Damascus had to say on the subject, except that there is a considerably heightened anti-Jewishness in Abū Qurrah's deployment of his master's argument that images are not idols. The adoration or the honor which one's act of *proskynēsis* (*as suǧūd*) expresses, Abū Qurrah contends, is addressed either to God, who deserves adoration, or to his saints who deserve honor. This practice is in accord with the actions of David, Solomon and other scriptural characters. Consequently, says Abū Qurrah, the scriptural prohibition of idolatry is addressed to the ancient Israelites, who had a constant proclivity to indulge in it, and not to the Christian practice of venerating images of Christ, and the saints, which is simply a way of giving adoration to God, to whom alone it is due, and honor to the saints, to whom it is appropriate[68].

Finally, at the end of the treatise Abū Qurrah takes up some particular challenges which the opponents employ in justifying their rejection of the veneration of images. It is a matter of applying the reasoning already elaborated earlier in the treatise to these specific objections, which are variations on the basic theme that venerating images is tantamount to idolatry.

The Text

Theodore Abū Qurrah's Arabic tract on the veneration of the holy icons first came to the notice of the modern world when John Arendzen, a priest of the Archdiocese of Westminster, published an

---

[68] In these chapters of his treatise, Abū Qurrah echoes many themes that seem first to have been sounded in Leontius of Neapolis' (d.c. 650) "Sermo Contra Judaeos." See *PG*, vol. 93, cols. 1597-1610; and Norman H. Baynes, "The Icons Before Iconoclasm," *Harvard Theological Review* 44 (1951), pp. 93-106.

edition together with a Latin translation, in 1897[69]. Arendzen's text is essentially a reproduction of the tract as it appears in the surviving copy, British Library Oriental MS 4950, written by Stephen of Ramlah, a monk of the monastery of Mar Charitōn in Palestine, who finished his work on 1 December 877[70]. The only other known copy of the tract is in a tenth century Arabic manuscript now in the possession of the monastery of St. Catherine at Mt. Sinai, Sinai Arabic MS 330 (ff. 315r-356r)[71]. It is an undated manuscript which the catalogers of the Sinai manuscripts have assigned to the tenth century on the basis of paleographical considerations[72]. In 1986, Ignace Dick, a priest of the Melkite Archdiocese of Aleppo, Syria, published a critical edition of the Arabic text of Abū Qurrah's work, based on the two surviving manuscripts[73]. Until recently the only translation of the text into a modern language was Georg Graf's German version of Arendzen's edition, which Graf published in 1910 together with translations of ten other Arabic treatises by Theodore Abū Qurrah, which Constantine Bacha had brought out some six years earlier. Now there is also an Italian translation of Dick's edition of the text[74].

The following English translation of Theodore Abū Qurrah's Arabic tract on the Christian practice of making prostration to the

[69] Johannes Arendzen, *Theodori Abū Kurra De cultu imaginum libellus a codice Arabico nunc primum editus Latine versus illustratus* (Bonn, 1897).

[70] See Sidney H. Griffith, "Stephen of Ramlah and the Christian Kerygma in Arabic in Ninth-Century Palestine," *Journal of Ecclesiastical History* 36 (1985), pp. 23-45.

[71] Ignace Dick published the notice of the additional copy of the tract in his article, "Deux écrits inédits de Théodore Abūqurra," *Le Muséon* 72 (1959), p. 54.

[72] A. S. Atiya, *The Arabic Manuscripts of Mount Sinai* (Baltimore, 1955), p. 9.

[73] Ignace Dick, *Théodore Abūqurra, Traité du culte des icônes* (PAC, 10; Jounieh, Rome, 1986).

[74] Georg Graf, *Die arabischen Schriften des Theodor Abu Qurra, Bischofs von Harrān (ca. 740-820)* (Paderborn, 1910), pp. 278-333; Contantin Bacha, *Les oeuvres arabes de Théodore Aboucara évêque d'Haran* (Beyrouth, 1904); P. Pizzo (ed. & trans.), *Teodoro Abu Qurrah, Difesa delle icone. Trattato sulla venerazione delle immagini* (Bibl. Vicino Oriente; Milano, 1995).

holy icons was made on the basis of the translator's collation of the
text of the work in B.L. Or. 4950, ff. 198r-237v and Sinai Arabic
MS 330 (Kamil, 457), ff. 315r-356r. Ignace Dick has now made available an Arabic edition of the tract, based on these two manuscripts.

The titles of the tract in the two manuscripts are as follows:

> A treatise which the holy Abba Theodore, bishop of Ḥarrān, Abū
> Qurrah wrote. In it he affirms that prostration to the icon of
> Christ, our God become incarnate from the Holy Spirit and from
> the immaculate Virgin Mary, as well as to the icons of his saints, is
> incumbent upon every Christian; also that in the case of a Christ-
> ian who disavows venerating these icons, his disavowal is due to
> ignorance of Christianity's present glory, and that if he takes this
> stand he must also disavow most of the mysteries of Christianity,
> the Christian's acceptance of which on right faith is from the holy
> apostles. (BL 4950, f. 198r.)
>
> This is a discourse that Theodore, the bishop of Ḥarrān, pro-
> nounced, in which he affirms that prostration to the icon of Christ,
> our God, become incarnate from the Holy Spirit, and from the
> immaculate virgin Mary, as well as of the icons of his saints, is
> incumbent upon every Christian. (Sinai 330, f. 315r).

It remains only to say that the "abstracts" which appear at the
heads of the chapters of Abū Qurrah's tract are present in both
manuscripts. This and other features of the text which will be
mentioned in the notes suggest that what we have before us is an
edited recension of the original work.

CHAPTER I

Abba Yannah, our brother, you who are here with us in Edessa,
have informed us that many Christians are abandoning the pros-

tration to the icon of Christ our God[75]. In his compassion, for the sake of our salvation, he made it possible for there to be an icon of him, due to his incarnation from the Holy Spirit and from the virgin Mary. The same too with the icons of his saints. In the Holy Spirit they were emboldened to enter into the arena to participate with him in his sufferings. By perseverance they enhanced the embellishment of his cross and became leaders[76] of honor for the believers, the memory of whom stirs them to imitate them, and to crowns of victory like theirs.

Anti-Christians, especially ones claiming to have in hand a scripture sent down from God[77], are reprimanding them for their prostration to these icons, and because of it they are imputing to them the worship of idols, and the transgression of what God commanded in the Torah and the Prophets, and they sneer at them.

You have asked us to compose a tract on this subject. In it we should return the reproach to those who reproach us for something in which there is no reproach. We should bring the hearts of

---

[75] On the identity of Abba Yannah, presumably an official at the church of the Icon of Christ in Edessa, see Sidney H. Griffith, "Theodore Abū Qurrah's Arabic Tract on the Practice of Venerating Images," pp. 58 & 59. The "icon of Christ our God" to which Abū Qurrah refers here is the famous acheiropoietos of Edessa. See Ernst von Dobschütz, *Christusbilder; Untersuchungen zur christlichen Legende (TU*, vol. XVIII; Leipzig, 1899), pp. 102-196; Averil Cameron, "The History of the Image of Edessa; the Telling of a Story," in *Okeanos; Essays Presented to Ihor Sevcenko, Harvard Ukrainian Studies* 7 (1983), pp. 80-94; J.-M. Fiey, "Image d'Edesse ou linceul de Turin, qu'est-ce qui a été transféré à Constantinople en 944?" *Revue d'Histoire Ecclésiastique* 82 (1987), pp. 271-277.

[76] The Arabic word here translated as "leaders" is the plural form of *imām*, the Islamic technical term for the leader of the community at prayer.

[77] The "anti-Christians" are Muslims and Jews, as will become clear as the text progresses. Here, the phrase "a scripture sent down from God" echoes the *Qur'ān*'s diction. Abū Qurrah uses the expression throughout the tract.

those frightened away from prostration to the holy icons back to the practice of prostration to them, in the orthodox way which our fathers established and approved. They were blessed in the Holy Spirit, who taught them heavenly wisdom, hidden in thick darkness from the minds of the wise men of the world, the best of whose wisdom is simple folly beside the lowest and the least of it.

I praise your solicitude, and I think it is appropriate to comply with your request, not in reliance on myself, that I should be able to set up the least goal for anyone of the Christians in his religion, or to protect them when anyone of the outsiders[78], people of perdition, error and rudeness, moves his tongue for Satan to cause them doubts. Rather, my reliance is on your prayers, which are no doubt not disdained by Christ. If for nothing else than for your affection for his church, ransomed by him through the shedding of his blood, and for the sake of your arousing us from the sleep of our own neglect, so that his wares might not go for nought, you deserve a ray of light to drive away from you the enveloping darkness of my own sinfulness.

CHAPTER II

Abstract: A person who refrains from making the prostration to the icons because of its repulsiveness to the outsiders must disregard other mysteries of Christianity too, because of their loathsomeness to these same people.

[78] Abū Qurrah uses the term *al-barrāniyyīn*, i.e., "outsiders," some nine times in the tract to designate Muslims and Jews. It is a transliteration of the Syriac word *barrānāyâ*, often used for "heathens" or even desert nomads. See R. Payne Smith, *Thesaurus Syriacus* (2 vols.; Oxford, 1879-1901), vol. I, col. 578.

First of all, I shall begin with amazement at those Christians in whose hearts the ridicule of strangers lodges, so that it turns them away from paying honor to the icons, and from making the prostration to them. How is it that they have not dealt similarly with any other part of integral Christianity because people vilify it, but they have remained complacent with it, even though people are quick to find it loathsome? Complacency with whatever else people find loathsome is not irrelevant to the notion that this practice is loathsome.

A sufficient indication of the sinfulness of these Christians, and of the deep-rootedness of the blindness in their minds, is the fact that they are not just, since even among themselves they do not deal equitably with equivalent things. Why do I say "equivalent"? Is there not more than this in Christianity that is much more abominable in the eyes of her opponents?

Who of these people, hearing Christians say that God has a son who is his equal, of his very being, would not say that they are mad? And when anyone hears them saying of this son born of God, God is not prior to him, will he not think them the contrariest of people? Their saying that the Father, the Son, and the Holy Spirit, each one of them is perfect God, and not three gods but one God, is this not for these people an instance of the onset of madness? When Christians speak of the descent of the eternal Son into the womb of Mary in the latter days, of his incarnation and birth from her, and then they proceed to talk of his progress from infancy, of his flight from Herod into Egypt, of his submission to his Father, his fasting and prayer, his request to his Father to make the cup, the cup of death, pass from him, of the Jews' arrest of him, of how they treated him, of their crucifixion of him, of his saying on the cross, "My God, my God, why have you forsaken me?" (Matt 27:46) — will not the outsiders think that they are only babbling, and that the babble of sleep is closer to right reason than their talk?

What do you think they will say when they see Christians bringing bread and wine to their altars, speaking some words over them, then receiving communion and saying this is Christ's flesh and his blood? They will see nothing is altered; it comes out just as it went in. When they see us pouring water into a basin, blessing it with words, then we immerse a man in it and bring him up out of it saying this man was old, and of a corrupt character before his baptism in this water, but now he has become young and of a sound character, after having been a son of the flesh — these and similar things are what scare them away from Christianity, and drive them far away from it.

Anyone of the Christians who is averse to the mania of the speech of these people, must renounce, in addition to the prostration to the holy icons, also the rest of Christianity we have mentioned because of their reproach. Indeed, not in vain did St. Paul say, "The word of the cross is foolishness to those passing away." (1 Cor 1:18) How could it not be foolishnesss to them? It contradicts what is right according to the minds of both their wise men and the ignorant. For this reason St. Paul went on to explain: "Where is the wise man, and where is the understanding man, and where is the disputant of this world? Has God not made the world's wisdom foolish? When by God's wisdom the world did not come to know God by wisdom, God wanted by the foolishness of the kerygma to bring to life those who would believe." (1 Cor 1:20-21)

CHAPTER III

Abstract: Christianity is a godly wisdom, which the minds of the wise men of the world call ignorance. Because, in their own ignorance, they suppose that their wisdom is the utmost of sagacity; they have given Christianity the name of foolishness because it contradicts their wisdom.

The proclamation of Christianity[79] is clearly given the name of foolishness. And it has been given such a name not because it is such, but only because the wisdom of the world has so named it. But the wisdom of the world did not give this proclamation the name of foolishness until God had called it foolish. And God's calling it foolish was only because it was superior, and the eminence of the minds of its adherents surpassed the minds of everyone else to whom people generally gave the name of wisdom. For when God revealed the proclamation of Christianity, and it was contradictory to their wisdom, beyond which they used to think there was no wisdom, it seemed right to them that it be given the name of foolishness — because everything contradictory to wisdom is foolishness.

As for the truth of the matter, the proclamation of Christianity is the true wisdom, compared with which the wisdom of the world is foolishness. As St. Paul said, "Among mature people we talk of a wisdom that is not like the wisdom of this world. Rather, we speak of God's wisdom in mystery." (1 Cor 2:6-7) And he also said, "The world's wisdom is foolishness with God." (1 Cor 3:19)

If this is so, Christians should certainly not disapprove of the people of the world calling their creed foolish. And they should understand that these people, in their foolishness, are calling Christianity foolish because it is the perfect wisdom, which their minds are prevented from attaining because it is attained only in

---

[79] Abū Qurrah's phrase is *da'watu n-naṣrāniyyah*, which is parallel to the Islamic expression, *da'watu l'islām*, the call to profess Islam. See M. Canard, "*Da'wa*," *EI*, new ed., Vol. II, pp. 168-170.

the Holy Spirit. As St. Paul said, "No one can say that Jesus is Lord except in the Holy Spirit."(1 Cor 12:3) And the Holy Spirit's descent is fitting only in connection with humility and the rejection of the prevailing pride.

No doubt everyone who is proficient in the wisdom of the world thinks there is no wisdom superior to it. As St. James the Apostle said, "Who is wise and knowledgeable among you? By good conduct let him show his excellence in the humility of wisdom. If in your hearts there is envy and bitter rivalry, do not boast against the truth. This wisdom does not come down from above. Rather, it is earthly, animalish, satanic." (Jas 3:13-15) Clearly, earthly wisdom is animalish, and the animalish person does not understand spiritual things. Rather for him spiritual things are foolishness. As St. Paul said, "We have not received the spirit of the world, but the spirit which is of God, to become acquainted with God's benefactions to us, of which we speak not by the tutelage of human wisdom's eloquence. Rather, by the tutelage of the Holy Spirit we are weighing out spiritual things to spiritual people. The animalish man is not receptive to the tutelage of the Holy Spirit, because for him it is foolishness." (1 Cor 2:12-14)

Therefore, the Christian should not disapprove of the outsiders' calling the spiritual, divine, heavenly mysteries of Christianity foolish. For, the most skilful of these people in their own wisdom is but someone animalish, satanic, utterly foolish. So it is not incumbent upon the Christians, on account of the prodding of someone like that, to hold themselves back from making prostration to the icon of Christ, our God incarnate, and to the icons of his saints. As we shall explain, God willing, they were established and became customary in the church by reason of the Holy Spirit.

CHAPTER IV

Abstract: We marvel at the outsiders; they believe in the scriptures of the Old [Testament], while they find fault with the mysteries of the Christians, due to the disapproval of the bodily-minded. With the same disapproval, the bodily-minded person disapproves of most of what is in their scriptures too, but they have no doubts about them.

The marvel of those outsiders who believe in some of the scriptures sent down from God, is the fact that in their own scriptures there are things similar to those features of Christianity, which the wise men of the world, whose minds are not at all submissive to faith, find even more foolish than they find those features to be foolish. The minds of these people have come to be satisfied with the very thing which they consider to be repulsive in Christianity, concomitant with their disapproval of the like of it in Christianity.

Would anyone whose mind is too haughty for faith not laugh when he hears that God created things out of nothing, and when he wants to make something he simply says to it "Be, and it becomes?" (*al-Baqarah*, II:117) Who of these people will not scoff when he hears that Eve came from Adam's rib? (Gen 2:21-22) How would it strike their minds for the scripture to say:

— that the serpent spoke; (Gen 3:1)
— that Balaam's ass held a conversation; (Num 22:28)
— that Lot's wife was changed into a pillar of salt; (Gen 19:26)
— that Moses' rod was changed into a serpent; (Exod 4:3)
— that Sarah, being barren, gave birth after she had become decrepit, from a man who had passed the point of being able to impregnate anyone; (Gen 18:11-12; 21:2)

— that the splitting of the sea and the gushing of streams of water out of the rock were due to Moses' rod; (Exod 14:21; 17:6)

— that a bush in which God was should catch fire but not be burned; (Exod 3:2)

— that men were thrown into the fiery furnace but were not burned; (Dan 3:24-25)

— that Jonah was in the belly of a whale for three days and three nights, and the whale spat him out alive and well; (Jon 1:7; 2:10)

— that Naaman the Syrian's leprosy came to a halt after his bath in the water of the Jordan at the word of Elisha the prophet; (2 Kgs 5:13-14)

— that wood sinks in water and iron floats; (2 Kgs 6:6)

— that there was a stopping of the sun and a resumption of its course; (Jos 10:12-13) and much more like this?

Would that I knew! Do the believers in these things not understand that the wise ones of the world, too proud for faith, will call them foolish for saying these things much more readily than they will call the Christians foolish for saying what they disavow? By right they should either not accept the like of what they disparage, or they should not disparage the like of what they accept.

CHAPTER V

Abstract: Things are said about God in the Old [Testament] that are more repugnant to minds devoid of faith than are those things said about Christ, because of which the people of the Old [Testament] maintain that he cannot possibly be God. A similar reproach is due to those other than the Jews who lay claim to faith.

The Christians hit the mark when they accept the Old [Testament] and the New [Testament], and understand them according to right meanings. Those who believe in the prophets, but consider what is in the Gospel wrong, ignore what the books of the prophets say about God himself. The bodily mind shudders uncontrollably to hear it.

Who of those with minds devoid of faith will accept the saying of scripture:

— that God walked in paradise; (Gen 3:8)
— that he smelt the aroma of a couple of pounds of fat and because of it became well pleased with this world; (Gen 8:21)
— that he regretted creating Adam; (Gen 6:6)
— that he came down to divide the tongues at Babel; (Gen 11:7)
— that he stopped over with Abraham, and ate and drank; (Gen 18)
— his saying to Abraham, "The clamor of Sodom has come up to me, so I came down in order to find out if the facts are in accord with what has reached me; if not, I will find out;" (Gen 18:20-21)
— that God stood atop a ladder and from there spoke with Jacob; (Gen 28:13)
— God's coming down onto Mount Sinai and his saying that "no one may see me and live," (Exod 33:20) and with that his conversation with Moses face to face, as a man converses with his companion;
— his coming down in a pillar of cloud to the Tent of Meeting; (Exod 40:34)
— Moses' saying that our God is "a consuming fire;" (Deut 4:24)

— also his saying that God marches in the encampment of the Israelites, and his prior notice to them to keep it clean of excrement for the sake of his marching in it; (Deut 23:12-15)

— Daniel's saying about God that he is "the ancient of days," and "his hair is like pure wool;" (Dan 7:9)

— Ezekiel's saying about him that he sits on a throne in the likeness of a man, and that from his waist up he is like lapis lazuli, and from his waist down fire; (Ezek 8:2)

— the prophet Amos' saying that he saw him standing at the edge of the river Mās[80];

— again, Ezekiel's saying that he married Jerusalem, and that she committed adultery against him, so he divorced her, but according to the prophet Hosea he promised her he would espouse her again; (Ezek 16 & Hos 2)

— and other things similar to these?

Should you not keep this in mind, O Jew, and cover your head before you mock the affairs of the Christians? If someone other than you of those who lay a claim to faith says that he will not accept any of this, he too no doubt says that God sits on a throne, (*Yūnus*, X:3) and he says God has hands and a face, (*Āl 'Imrān*, III:73; *ar-Rūm*, XXX:38) and other such things that we cannot be bothered to pursue here. When he imputes bodiliness to God in these statements, then willy nilly he makes it permissible for God to be spoken of in terms of other bodily appendages as well. Whether he maintains that this sort of attribute is only applied to God plainly, and not according to some figure of

---

[80] There is no such passage in the book of Amos. Perhaps Abū Qurrah is referring to Dan 10:4 and/or 12:6.

speech, or he says that is said of God according to some fit figure of speech, he nevertheless thereby allows other things, of which he disapproves, also to be said of God according to some fit meaning. And this pronouncement goes for the Jews and anyone else who lays claim to faith, in what concerns them about God's attributes[81].

So how can you think it is right to accuse the Christians for something that in your own case is comparable to it, or even more repugnant, except out of rudeness or boorishness?

As for us Christians, by the grace of the Holy Spirit we believe in the Old [Testament] and in the New [Testament], and we know that their starting point and their route are one; we understand everything in them from its point of view. In our own minds we accord God the purest attributes, but we also recognize his descent, in his mercy, into something other than what is in harmony with the transcendence of his being — wherein is our salvation, for which we thank him.

The marvel of our own ignoramuses is that were it not for the Christians, by the subtlety of their spiritual minds, presenting the scriptures of the Jews in a favorable light, they would have become a laughing stock for all people. And the Jews have no doubt about it because people do call them foolish. So, will they turn their faces away from making prostration to the holy icons because the Jews and others find them repugnant?

[81] Here and elsewhere in the tract Abū Qurrah addresses his remarks to a Jew, or the Jews, even when, as in the present paragraph, he is quoting from the *Qur'ān*, and speaking of Muslims, the "other people who lay claim to faith." In the Islamic milieu in which he wrote, Abū Qurrah avoided direct references to Muslims. Like other defenders of the icons, however, he frequently directs his arguments against the Jews, who were widely charged with being at the root of hostility to icons in the Christian community.

CHAPTER VI

Abstract: Christianity was accepted only because of miracles, but God will unceasingly raise up for her those who will vouch for her from reason.

In all that he professes, every Christian must take a firm stand on the insight of faith. Surely every one of the Christians to do so knows that for those accepting it, Christianity was proved true only by the miracles that the disciples worked in the name of Jesus Christ. Thereby reason judged correctly that they deserved that everything that they taught should be accepted. At the same time, there is the testimony of the prophets to what they proclaimed of Christ's career — the prophets, whose scriptures are in the possession of the Jews, the enemies of their preaching. The same may be said for what the minds of some philosophers used to study, men deserving of recompense from God for their search for the truth with a just intention, of the subtlest of which men such as Dionysius, Clement, Hierotheos, and their like, used to read and write[82].

We too, bold as we are, have composed treatises; from the details we have gleaned from our holy fathers we have proved that there is today no scripture at all affirmed by reason except the Gospel[83]. Everything the Gospel affirms, because of the Gospel's

---

[82] The references are to Dionysius the Areopagite, whom Abū Qurrah thought to be the author of the texts modern scholars ascribe to a now anonymous fifth century writer, who is aptly called Pseudo-Dionysius, Clement of Alexandria (d.c. 215 A.D.), and the Hierotheos to whom Pseudo-Dionysius often refers as his master.

[83] A reference to another work by Abū Qurrah, published in the original Arabic and translated into French by Constantin Bacha, *Un traité des oeuvres arabes de Théodore About-Kurra, évêque de Harran; publié et traduit en français pour la première fois* (Tripoli de Syrie & Rome, 1905).

affirmation of it, is to be accepted. Incumbent upon people is conviction about everything in the Gospel, whether their own minds have become aware of it or not. And we know that the Holy Spirit will continue to bring out from among the Christians those who will weigh out spiritual things to spiritual men, as St. Paul says. (Cf. 1 Cor 2:13)

We are constrained by the rule of reason to consent to everything pertaining to Christianity, which we mentioned above that the Jews and others, in the blindness of their minds, find repulsive. Anyone who has not attained the stature of a man in understanding spiritual things, must build on the foundation of faith and submit to whatever has become current practice in the church from the apostles, in the matter of the prostration made to the holy icons, or anything else. In faith there is insight. On the other hand, if one undertakes to accept some of it, whereas what he accepts and what he rejects is one in the bodily mind's disapproval of it, then he proves it against himself that he has no insight in his religion, and that he does not know for what reason he persists in it.

CHAPTER VII

Abstract: Proof that the icons have a firm basis in Christianity because of their ubiquity in all the churches. Anyone who disavows making prostration to them because he cannot cite for it any of the messengers[84] in the books of the Old [Testament] or

---

[84] The Arabic term here translated "messengers" is *ar-rusul*, the plural form of the noun *ar-rasūl*, which is the Qur'ān's term for Moses, Jesus, Muḥammad, and others of God's "messengers" who in the Islamic view have brought scriptures from God to the human community.

the New [Testament], must also disavow other mysteries of Christianity that are like it.

Maybe someone of those people will say, "How can we know that making the prostration to the icons grew up in the church at the commission of the apostles, since we cannot find a scripture to speak of it?" We shall say to him that there is much of great moment in our possession that we got by right, that has come down to us only as an inheritance, without our being able to find a firm basis for it in any of the books of the Old [Testament] or the New [Testament], which the disciples handed on to us. The first thing is the formula (*al-kalām*) we say over our Eucharistic offering, by which it becomes the flesh of Christ, and his blood. then there is the liturgy of Baptism and of the Chrism; the consecration of sanctuaries; ordination; striking the semantron; the veneration of the cross, and similar things.

Whoever will not accept from us the practice of making prostration to the icons of the saints, until he finds a firm basis for it in the canonical books of the Old [Testament] and the New [Testament], will have to discontinue everything else we have mentioned as well. So let him consider what sort of Christianity would then remain in his possession. If he accepts all but the practice of making prostration to the icons, in the same way let him accept prostration to the icons. He should know that of all these sorts of things, nothing is more prevalent in the church than the icons. What country is there, by my life, in whose churches there are no icons of the saints? If their ubiquity does not prove that they have come down from the beginning, then one is on the verge of disapproving everything else, the ubiquity of which is commonplace, claiming that it is adventitious.

If such a breach should be broken into Christianity, she would completely disappear. Far be it from Christ so to desert her! This should be enough to say to those who are shying away from making prostration to the holy icons, to bring them back to what they have relinquished.

CHAPTER VIII

Abstract: Testimony from the teachers to prove that the icons are in the church at the commission of the apostles, and that to make prostration to them is obligatory. Furthermore, that the rank of the teachers is firmly fixed high up in the church, and that Christians must without fail obey them.

If, in spite of it all, you want to know that making prostration to the icon of Christ, and to the icons of the saints, is a fundamental principle in God's church, listen to what the well-known St. Athanasius says about it in the *Questions* which Duke Antiochus asked him about some things in connection with which he thought the church had some inconsistency. St. Athanasius is the first among the teachers, the possessor of five crowns in the fight for orthodoxy, the strongest pillar of the church[85].

Antiochus asked, what business is it of ours to make prostration to the icons and to the cross? They are the handiwork of carpenters, like the idols. In the prophets God gave the command that we should not make prostration to the works of human hands.

---

[85] St. Athanasius' (d. 373) five crowns are the five exiles he endured. The work to which Abū Qurrah here refers, the so-called *Quaestiones ad Antiochum Ducem*, is included among the spurious compositions attributed to St. Athanasius in *PG*, vol. XXVIII, cols. 597-709. See the comments of G. Bardy, "La littérature patristique des "Quaestiones et Responsiones," sur l'écriture sainte," *Revue Biblique* 42 (1933), pp. 328-332.

In answer to him St. Athanasius said that for us believers, making prostration to God is not the same as making prostration to the icons; it is not like worshipping idols. Rather, with our prostration to icon or to cross, we undertake only to show love and affection for the person whose icon it is. For this reason, whenever the icon is effaced, what was once an image is then most frequently burnt as firewood. Again, just as Jacob, when he came near death, bowed down on the top of Joseph's staff, he did not do so to honor the staff, but the one who was holding the staff in his hand. (See Gen 47:31 LXX, Pesh.; Heb. 11:21) So too we believers, for no other reason do we show honor to images and come to touch them. It is like kissing sons and fathers, to show the love for them we have within us. So too did the Jew in times gone by make prostration to the tablets of the Law and the Cherubim cast in gold; he was not showing honor to the nature of gold or stone, but to the Lord; he ordered it to be made[86].

As for those people who, due to the dullness of their minds, presumptuously refuse to make prostration to the cross and the likenesses of the saints, let them tell us why it is that from images, icons of the saints, by the power of God the Omnipotent, oil oftentimes flows. How does an inanimate, upright stele, pierced by an arrow, flow with a miraculous flow of blood like something of the nature of flesh? How do graves, bones and icons of the saints oftentimes drive out demons with shouts and wailing? Let us not disabuse these ignorant people with just talk, but with the reports of the fathers.

---

[86] See *Quaestiones ad Antiochum Ducem*, no. 39, *PG*, vol. XXVIII, col. 621. St. John of Damascus quoted this passage, also attributing it to St. Athanasius. See B. Kotter (ed.), *Die Schriften des Johannes von Damaskos* (vol. III, *Contra Imaginum Calumniatores Orationes Tres*; Berlin & New York, 1975), pp. 169 & 191.

Listen to a credible saying that has come down to us from the fathers of Jerusalem in a report about an icon. On the word of people worthy of credence, who lived in times past, there was one of the religious men whom the demon of fornication used to trouble; it would upset him severely. One day that spirit appeared to him face to face and said to him, "If you want me not to fight with you, then do not keep making prostration to this certain icon, and I shall stay away from you." The icon was the icon of our Lady, the mother of God, St. Mary[87].

Would that I knew what to say about those who avoid [the practice], and who give us orders not to make prostration to the images, the icons of the saints that are drawn and copied among us only for a memorial and for nothing else. This, in brief, is what to say about icons and images. As for the cross, it is well known that we make prostration to it, and we believers salute it only for the sake of Christ, who was crucified on it. This is the doctrine of St. Athanasius.

As for Eusebius, the bishop of Caesarea in Palestine, the one who wrote the history of the church from the birth of our Saviour in Bethlehem up to the time of the great king, Constantine; in the seventh book, the seventeenth chapter [sic], he mentions the woman whom our Lord healed of the flow of blood. He maintains she was from Paneas. About her Eusebius says:

> Since we have mentioned this city, we should not pass over a story that deserves to be a keepsake for those who come after us. They claim that the woman whose flow of blood we know about from

[87] John of Damascus also tells this story, attributing it to Sophronius, the patriarch of Jerusalem (d. 638). See Kotter, *Contra Imaginum Calumniatores*, p. 124. The story actually comes from the *Leimonarion* of John Moschus (d. 619). See M.-J. Rouet de Journel, *Jean Moschus, Le Pré Spirituel* (Paris, 1946), pp. 89-90.

the holy Gospel, the one whom our Lord cured of this malady, was
from this city, and her house is well known in the city. Moreover,
there is a miraculous sign which remains until today of the benefit
that came to her from our Lord. Before the door of her house there
is a bronze image in the likeness of a woman, and the image is
kneeling, on its knees, its hands extended, beseeching in the manner of that woman whose blood flowed, whom our Lord Jesus
Christ cured. Opposite there is a bronze image like a man standing
upright, wrapped in a cloak, stretching out his hand to this woman.
From under the foot of this image there grows up over the stele the
strangest of herbs in appearance, reaching up to the top of his
cloak, and it is a remedy for every ailment. The likeness is in resemblance to our Saviour. It has lasted until our own days, and we have
seen it with our own eyes when we went to this city. It is not surprising that the artisans were those of the gentiles to have benefited
from our Saviour, since we see them already having made color portraits of the apostles, St. Paul and St. Peter. And of Christ himself
there remain icons until this very day[88].

Does Eusebius not verify for you that these likenesses and icons
have continually been in the possession of Christians since the
time of the apostles? By my life, the proof of what he says is the
fact that the icon that portrays the apostles remains until today, as
does the icon of Christ. Indeed, these icons were authenticated by
the very countenances of the apostles in person, and by the countenance of Christ. St. Athanasius gave the recommendation to
make prostration to them; he reported that they were antiques

---

[88] Abū Qurrah has the chapter number wrong; it is Book VII, chap. 18. See
G. Bardy, *Eusèbe de Césarée, Histoire Ecclésiastique; livres V-VII* (SC, n. 415; Paris,
1955), pp. 191-192. John of Damascus also quoted this chapter from Eusebius'
Ecclesiastical History. See Kotter, *Contra Imaginum Calumniatores*, p. 173. However, Abū Qurrah left out the last phrases, and he even changed the meaning of
the final sentence. Eusebius disdained the whole business as a remnant of what
he called, "*ethnike synetheia.*" Abū Qurrah, unlike John of Damascus, omits this
phrase, and thereby suggests Eusebius' approval of the images in Paneas.

even before his time. So this is a strict command for every Christian, no doubt about it, because he is the chief of the teachers, none of whom is more eminent than he.

St. Gregory the Theologian, in the homily he preached on Christ's birthday, gives you the order to make a prostration to the manger which was a kind of cradle for our Lord. And he also gives you the order to make a prostration to the rock, because of its connection with Christ[89], to whom every act of prostration is necessarily due — contrary to your foolish statement that one is not permitted to make an act of prostration to anything except to God.

After these two teachers[90], whom no one surpasses, understand that teachers have a high rank in the church, above all the ranks after the rank of the apostles and the prophets. As St. Paul said, "God put the apostles first in his church, after them the prophets, and after them the teachers." (1 Cor 12:28) Thereafter in the first ranks, workers of miracles come first, and then those after them. Since they have this eminence in the church, what Christian can repudiate anything of their teaching without becoming a renegade from Christianity, someone debarred from the fold of the church? For what the apostles and prophets said bears a resemblance to the

---

[89] An allusion to Gregory of Nazianzus' *Oratio* XXXVIII, "In Theophania, sive Nathalitia Salvatoris," *PG*, vol. XXXVI, col. 332A. However, there is no reference in this sermon to the rock Abū Qurrah mentions. Georg Graf supposed the rock was one on which the child Jesus lay. See Graf, *Die arabischen Schriften*, p. 292, n.2.

[90] Athanasius and Eusebius were the two teachers first quoted in this chapter. The reference to "two teachers" here doubtless refers to them. Mention of Gregory the Theologian was probably inserted later, perhaps by someone other than Abū Qurrah. This intrusion, plus such editorial refinements as the "Abstract" at the head of each chapter, suggests that Abū Qurrah's tract on the icons received some revision between its composition and its reproduction in the two manuscript copies we have of it.

wheat from which people get no benefit as long as it is whole. The teachers resemble a man whose business is with the wheat; he grinds it, he kneads it, he makes baked bread out of it. He brings out its potentiality, hidden from anyone who sees it whole, who has had no practical experience with it. When he has prepared it, one may get the benefit of it. For this reason, God dignified their rank, and named them fathers to the believers.

A sufficient consolation for any Christian who makes prostration to the holy icons is to know that in his practice of making prostration to them he is following the teachers. Enough for those dull-minded people, who out of shame avoid making the prostration, is their being at variance with them; it is what proves against them the disavowal of Christianity as a whole. And for us, this is really the standard by which we would bring back the Christians altogether to the practice of making prostration to these icons.

CHAPTER IX

Abstract: An argument against the outsiders, and their offering as a pretext God's saying, "You shall not make for yourself likenesses, nor shall you make prostration to them." (See Exod 20:4-5; Deut 5:8-9) Proof that it is not God's will that no prostration be made to anything other than to him.

I know that all the children of the church are anxious to hear us arguing on this subject with those who are dead because of their being at variance with Christianity. There do exist Christians who, because of their promotion of prostration to the icons of the saints, have surpassed death. So it is appropriate for us to do something to put forward for our brothers a masterpiece with which we might make them happy, if we have the ability for it in the Holy Spirit. We have not looked for our own sinfulness, nor set forth our own wishes for our own profit, albeit that poverty will have made it impossible for us to carry out our desires.

So, with God's help, we shall begin our controversy with these people by saying to them, "Tell us where you get your rebuke to us for making prostration to the icon of Christ our Lord, and to the icons of his saints." They will say, "From God's saying in the Torah":

> I am the Lord your God who brought you out from the land of Egypt, from the abode of slavery; you shall not have gods beside me, nor shall you make for your self an idol, or a likeness of anything in the heavens above, or of anything on the earth below, or of anything in the water beneath the earth. You shall not make prostration to them, nor shall you serve them. I am the Lord, your God. (Exod 20:2-5)

There is also what Moses said in Deuteronomy:

> To the Lord your God shall you make prostration; him alone shall you serve. (Deut 6:13, as in Matt 4:10, Luke 4:8)

And in the prophets he was continually angry at the Israelites because they were making prostration to idols and to images.

In answer we say to them, it is true that he gave the commandment you have quoted; nothing would hinder you from collecting many similar testimonies. But tell us, by his saying, "You shall not make prostration," did he intend simply that there should be none other than himself to whom prostration is made? If you say this, you will have turned the holy fathers and the prophets into sinners! How will you deal with Abraham, God's friend? (see Isa 41:8; Jas 2:23; *an-Nisa'*, IV:125) He made a prostration to the sons of Heth when he asked them to sell him a grave in which he

could bury Sarah. (see Gen 23:7) Seven times Jacob made prostration on the ground to his brother Esau. (see Gen 33:3) Joseph's
brothers prostrated themselves to Joseph, faces to the ground. (see
Gen 42:6) Israel made a prostration to Joseph on the top of his
staff. (see Gen 47:31 LXX, Pesh.; Heb. 11:21) Joseph's two sons
prostrated themselves to their grandfather Israel, their faces to the
ground. (see Gen 48:12 LXX, Pesh.) Moses made a prostration to
his father-in-law. (Exod 18:7)

Perhaps someone will say, "this practice of prostration of which
you speak was only prior to God's command that no prostration
be made to anything other than to himself."

We say, regarding Moses' act of prostration to the father-in-law,
that God's teaching him the Law came prior to it — on the occasion when he commanded him to sweeten the bitter water with
the stick of wood. During the Exodus of the Israelites, so it is
written in the Torah, Moses cried out to the Lord and the Lord
showed him a stick of wood. He threw it into the water, and the
water became sweet. It was there God gave him the statutes and
ordinances. (see Exod 15:25-26)

We should also call your attention to what was done after God
commanded that no prostration be made to anything other than
to himself, as you say.

— Did not the mother of Solomon, David's son, make a prostration to David? (see 1 Kgs 1:16)
— Did not the prophet Nathan come into David's presence, and
   bow down with his face to the ground, and make a prostration
   to him? (see 1 Kgs 1:23)
— In the book of Kings it says that Bathsheba knelt down with
   her face to the ground, and prostrated herself to the king. (see
   1 Kgs 1:31)

— Adoniah, David's son, made a prostration to Solomon. (see 1 Kgs 1:53)
— When Solomon's mother came into his presence, to beseech him in Adoniah's behalf, the king stood up before her and made a prostration to her. (see 1 Kgs 2:19)
— It says in the book of Paralipomena that king David said to the whole assembly, "Glorify the Lord, our God," and the entire assembly gave glory to the Lord, the God of their fathers, and they dropped down onto their knees, and made a prostration to God and to the king. (see 1 Chr 29:20)
— Even the sons of the prophets, did they not make prostration to the ground, to Elisha the prophet? (see 2 Kgs 2:15)

All of this proves, O Jew, that if it had been God's will that absolutely no prostration be made to anything other than to himself, all of these prophets would have become sinners. Far be it from God that they should have done so! Furthermore, you would be putting God into contradiction to himself if you reduce to your own idea the saying of his we have quoted, in which he gave instruction to the Israelites. Indeed, by way of prophecy, Isaac gave a blessing to Jacob and said to him, "Chieftains will make prostration to you, and your own father's sons will prostrate themselves to you." (Gen 27:29 LXX only)

Now, O Jew, if you want this saying to apply to Jacob himself, so take it. But if you want it to apply to Christ, we shall have no quarrel with you here[91]. However you take it, by my life, it invalidates your opinion, since it is your idea that Christ is not God, but simply a man.

Similarly, Jacob made a prophecy about Judah, meaning Christ. He said to him, "Your relatives will make prostration to you."

---

[91] Christians sometimes consider Jacob to be a type for Christ.

(Gen 49:8) And David prophesied about Christ, "All the kings [of the earth] will make prostration to him." (Ps 72:11 LXX, Pesh.) So tell us, O Jew, are you going to make Christ God, since on God's orders he deserves prostration from all people? Then you will have become a Christian. Or will you say that Christ is a man, since you know now that it is not God's will that no prostration be made to anything other than to him? Rather, he only forbade making prostration to the idols, the gods of the gentiles. At that time they were the ones who were satans, according to what David the prophet says, "All the gods of the gentiles are satans." (Ps 96:5 — "satans" for LXX *daimonia*)

Understand that performing the act of prostration is sometimes by way of worship, and sometimes by way of something other than worship. There are people other than you, O Jew, among those who say that it is not permissible to make an act of prostration except to God. They too mock the Christians for their practice of making prostration to the icons and to people. they maintain that making the act of prostration is worship, all the while having it in mind that "God commanded all the angels to prostrate themselves to Adam, and they prostrated themselves, except Iblis refused, and came to be among the unbelievers." (*al-Baqarah* II:34) If prostration is an act of worship, then without a doubt, according to what you say, God in that case commanded the angels to worship Adam! Far be it from God to do that!

Should one not then understand that the practice of making prostration is sometimes by way of honor? One should refrain from mocking the Christians when he sees them making prostration to their bishops, and he should bear it in mind that he too says that Jacob and his sons "bowed down as ones making prostration (*sujjadan*)" to Joseph. (*Yūsuf*, XII:100) So he certainly should not find fault with anyone who does what the prophets did.

This goes for the Jew, and for anyone else, — to affirm that it is not God's will that no prostration be made to anything other than to him. It is the crowning glory of Christianity, that not being in contradiction to God, she permits her people to make prostration to others than to God.

CHAPTER X

Abstract: It is not God's will that believers in Him are not to make for themselves likenesses or icons. A rebuke is due to those who say that whoever makes a portrait of anything living will be required on resurrection day to blow the spirit into its portrait.

In the Law God said:

> Do not make for yourself a reproduction of anything in heaven above, or on the earth below, or in the waters under the earth. (Exod 20:4)

By this he did not mean that people should not make portraits of anything in heaven or on earth or in the water. Whoever maintains that he meant just this, will have instantly put God into contradiction to himself, since he commanded Moses to make the Tent of Meeting as a reproduction, after the likeness of what he showed him on the mountain. He told him:

> Make a holy place for me, so that I might appear among you. Make a likeness of everything I showed you on the mountain, a reproduction of the Tent, and reproduction of its vessels; so shall you do. (Exod 25:8-9)

In another place he told him: "You shall make it according to what you saw on the mountain. So shall you do." (Exod 25:40) These things God commanded you to make, as you may see.

If you want to know that God as a matter of fact did order you to make faces and other bodily members, listen to what sort of thing it is he says to Moses. He said to him: "Make two hammered cherubim of gold, and put them at the sides of the propitiatory." (Exod 25:18) A little farther on he says:

> Let the Cherubim spread out their wings above, overshadowing the Propitiatory with their wings, and let their faces be turned toward one another over the Propitiatory, so that the faces of the Cherubim are facing one another. (Exod 25:20)

Notice that God commanded Moses to make faces and wings, perfect likenesses, as a reproduction of what He had shown him on the mountain. Therefore, in his saying to Israel, "Do not make for yourself a reproduction of anything in heaven, or on the earth, or in the water," (Exod 20:4) he did not mean that believers in him should not make for themselves any reproductions or likenesses at all. Rather, he forbade them only the reproductions which they used to make and to worship; these used to draw them away from the knowledge of God and his worship.

Solomon, David's son, likewise made Cherubim when he built God's house in Jerusalem, to become for him there what the Tent of Meeting had been in the desert. Their wings, their faces, and their feet are mentioned in the book of Paralipomena. (2 Chr 3:10-13) God also commanded Moses to make a serpent of bronze. (Num 21:8) In the temple Solomon made images of palm trees and lilies, and he made likenesses of a lion and of oxen. In the temple he also put a sea of cast bronze, that he set up on twelve oxen. (1 Kgs 7:19, 23, 25, 29, 36) In a vision God informed Ezekiel about the construction of the temple, that on its walls, inside and out, he should put hammered Cherubim, and palm trees. Each cherub had a face, and there was also the face of a lion. The whole temple, on every side, from the floor to the ceiling, was covered with cherubim and palm trees. (Ezek 41:15-20) All of these things are reproductions and likenesses of what is in heaven, or on the earth.

Where are those who say that on resurrection day, whoever has made a portrait, a likeness of anything living, will be required to blow the spirit into it[92]? Do you think that Solomon and Moses will be required to blow the spirit into these likenesses they made? God would then have willed them evil when he allowed the two of them to make them. Far be it from God to will evil on his friends!

The marvel of those who say this is that they themselves make pictures of plants, but they do not understand that if portrayers of living things will be required to blow spirits into what they have portrayed, they too are to be required to inspire their pictures and to make them grow, to produce fruit. Both things are one and the same in terms of human ability. It would be necessary for these people to be punished forever for their making pictures of plants, since they would be incapable of making these pictures as we have prescribed; their own judgment is operative against themselves, not against us[93].

---

[92] Abū Qurrah is here quoting a famous Islamic tradition reporting a saying of Muḥammad. See M. L. Krehl (ed.), *Le Recueil des traditions mahométanes par Abou Abdallah Mohammed ibn Ismail el-Bokhari* (4 vols.; Leyde, 1862-1908), vol. II, pp. 40-41. See Rudi Paret, "Die Entstehungszeit des islamischen bilderverbots," *Kunst des Orients* 11 (1976/77), pp. 158-181; Daan van Reenen, "The Bilderverbot, a New Survey," *Der Islam* 67 (1990), pp. 27-77, esp. pp. 44-45.

[93] Abū Qurrah would have had every opportunity to see images of trees and plants in the decorative programs of Islamic religious premises. See, e.g., M. Gautier — Van Berchem, "The Mosaics of the Dome of the Rock in Jerusalem and of the Great Mosque in Damascus," in K.A.C. Creswell, *Early Muslim Architecture, Umayyads A.D. 622-750* (2nd ed.; Oxford, 1969), vol. I, part 1, esp. pp. 246-290.

According to the scope of their own acceptation, they must understand that by their making pictures of plants they are at variance with God's saying in the Law, "Do not make for yourself a reproduction of anything in heaven, or on earth, or in the waters under the earth." (Exod 20:4) As a matter of fact, God did not say, "You shall not make for yourself a reproduction of anything living." Rather, all kinds of reproductions are included. So they are blaming others for the like of what they do themselves, but they take no notice of it.

We have clearly explained two things. When he said to Israel: "Do not make for yourself a reproduction of anything in heaven, or of anything on earth, or of anything in the waters under the earth, do not make prostration to them nor worship them;" (Exod 20:2-5) it was not God's will that believers not make icons or likenesses; nor that no prostration be made to anything other than to him.

They are unmasked who mock the Christians for putting icons of Christ and their saints in their churches, and for making prostration to people.

CHAPTER XI

Abstract: The definition of the act of prostration. One must make an act of prostration before the icons, and touch them in the prostration. God used to appear to the prophets only in representations.

Someone may say, "You have put the practice of installing icons in churches in a good light, and the practice of making prostration to people too. so tell us how you will make it seem right to make prostration to these icons." To this person we shall say that the act of prostration proves to be both by way of worship, and by way of non-worship. One of the ways of the prostration of non-worship is the way of honor[94].

Next we shall ask him, "Tell us, do you make the act of prostration only to the thing on which you put your knees and forehead, or to what your intention wills in putting down your knees and forehead in the act of making a bow[95]"?

If he were to say that the act of prostration is only to what the knees and the forehead touch, or to something comparable to what the knees and forehead of the person making prostration touch when he bends over, or to the nearest wall, or something else he faces when he makes the bow in prostration, his legal case is actionable against himself, not against us. This is what is to be reckoned blameworthy, that anyone would present himself as someone who unfailingly and continually makes prostration to any such things as these we have mentioned. It is the most reprehensible opinion anyone could hold about the practice of making prostration; its proponent should more appropriately be a beast!

It is inevitable that the act of prostration goes to what the intention has in mind in the flexing of the knees, putting down the forehead, and the direction one faces. Since this is so, anyone with a question should understand that Jacob made a prostration

---

[94] One recognizes here St. John of Damascus' distinction between the prostrations of adoration and of honor. See Kotter, *Contra Imaginum Calumniatores*, p. 87.

[95] Here Abū Qurrah is referring at least in part to the formal Islamic ritual of *ṣalāt*, which involves an act of prostration (*as-sajdah, as-sujūd*), often performed on a "prayer-rug", aptly called in Arabic, *as-sajjādah*. The statement of intention (*an-niyyah*, the word Abū Qurrah uses in this paragraph for "intention") is a formal element of the ritual procedure. See A. J. Wensinck, "*Sadjdjāda*," and "*Ṣalāt*," *EI*, vol. IV, pp. 47-51, 102.

on Joseph's staff, intending thereby to honor Joseph. (Gen 47:31 LXX) Moses used to make prostration in front of hammered figures of faces, with wings and other things that human hands had made; his prostration referred only to what he had in mind for it, and not to the image or item of manufacture before him. So too we Christians, when we make prostration in front of an icon of Christ or of the saints, our prostration is certainly not to the panels or the colors. Rather, it is only to Christ, to whom every kind of act of prostration is due, and to the saints to whom it is due by way of honor.

When the Israelites were at Jericho, after having been routed before their enemies, Joshua the son of Nun tore his garments and bowed down to the ground on his face in front of the ark of the Lord until evening, both he and the elders of Israel. There he made supplication to the Lord. (Jos 7:6) When he did it, he was only following the example of Moses, because of what God had said to Moses, "From there I shall be known to you." (Exod 25:22)

This was the practice of all the saints, to make prostration toward the place from which he would come to be known to people, although they had no doubt that he is in every place. As David said, "I shall make prostration to your holy temple, in fear of you." (Ps 5:8) He also said, "I lift up my hands to your holy temple." (Ps 28:2) And he said, "Let us prostrate ourselves in the place in which his feet stood." (Ps 132:7) Daniel, when he was in Babylon, simply opened the windows in his upper room in the direction of Jerusalem, to make prostration toward Jerusalem. (Dan 6:10) That was because he had heard in the Psalms that God chose Sion and wanted her to become his dwelling. He said, "She is my abode forever; here I shall dwell because I have loved her." (Ps 132:14)

Obviously the saints were making prostration only to God, in the direction of the place from which he would come to be known, although they knew no place could confine him. As it says in the Torah, during the Exodus of the Israelites, when Moses took a tent and pitched it outside of their camp, whenever he went out of the camp to the tent, all of the Israelites stood up to watch him, each one at the door of his own tent, until he would go into the tent. When Moses entered his tent, a pillar of cloud would come down to stand at the door of the tent, and from there God would speak with him. The entire people used to see the pillar of cloud standing at the door of the tent. And the entire people would stand up and make prostration, each one at the door of his own tent. (Exod 33:7-10)

Obviously, it was only to God to whom the Israelites were making prostration in the direction of the pillar, because he was speaking with Moses from the pillar of cloud. It was not unknown to their intelligentsia that God was not confined to that pillar; their prostration was accepted according to the mode of their intention's purpose. So how could it not be acceptable for Christians to face an icon of Christ, or of his saints, each one according to the way it merits[96]?

If anyone says that Christians are not content with the act of prostration in front of these icons until they touch them in the process of making the prostration, he should recall what we quoted earlier about Jacob's making prostration on Joseph's staff and his touching it in the process of his prostration. (Gen 47:31) There was conveyed only what was in accord with what he willed — to honor Joseph. One should also recall what we said about everyone who makes a prostration to God; his two knees touch but the

---

[96] Concern for the *qiblah*, the proper direction to face in prayer, is what concerns Abū Qurrah in these paragraphs. It was a major concern for Muslims, and it became a point to discuss in the inter-confessional dialogues of the period. See A. J. Wensinck, "*Kibla*," *EI*, new edition, vol. V, p. 83.

ground or a carpet, yet his prostration is conveyed only according to what he intends — to make an act of prostration to God.

It is the same with the Christians; their touching the icon in the process of their making the act of prostration is in accordance with what they want to do — to honor Christ, their God, or his saints, or the prophets, or the apostles, or the martyrs, or someone else.

Those whom we have mentioned were not the only ones who used to make prostration toward icons that had faces. Ezekiel, when he saw the chariot of fire, maintained that on it there were the face of a man; the face of a lion, the face of a bull, and the face of an eagle. (Ezek 1:10, 15) Above this there was the representation of a throne, and above the throne one with the appearance of a man. (Ezek 1:26) Then Ezekiel said, "This is the representation of the glory of the Lord. I looked, and I bowed down on my face." (Ezek 1:28) He repeated this a number of times in his book.

Obviously, God's prophet Ezekiel bowed down as one making prostration before the representation of the glory of God, on which there were these different faces. Therefore, no one should disallow the Christians to make the prostration to the icon of Christ, or of his saints, when they want to do what the prophets used to want to do in their act of prostration in front of images or representations. Certainly no one can contest it by supposing that Ezekiel used to think that the representation he saw was of the actual being of God, and for this reason he used to bow down on his face in its presence! Truly that would be to make different gods, or to make a single god that in his essence would change from one state of being to another. For Daniel saw God in yet a different appearance, and so did Isaiah. Rather, Ezekiel did as a matter of fact know that what he saw was a representation, just as he named it.

Far be it from the holy prophets that their thinking about God should be anything like what we have just mentioned! David the prophet danced before the ark of God when he transferred it to the tent he had prepared for it. (2 Sam 6:14) The Levites whom David appointed used to give praise and play on musical instruments in its presence. David and the other prophets were not honoring this ark by making the act of prostration in front of it, or by dancing a singing "Glory". But they were honoring something latent that they were imagining in their minds. The ark was its icon. As we stated in the beginning, God told Moses to make it as one of the appurtenances of the Tent of Testimony, as a reproduction of the model he showed him on the mountain. (Exod 25:8-9)

Therefore, no one should disallow the Christians to imagine Christ and his saints in their minds, and then to give them honor in their icons, just as the prophets used to show honor to the model in its icon evident to the eye. One should know that God appeared to the prophets only in representations, not in the actuality of being. Listen to him telling Moses, "No man sees me and lives." (Exod 33:20) Listen to Isaiah saying, "I have seen the king, Sabbaoth, the Lord, with my own eyes." (Isa 6:5) Again, listen to God saying in Hosea the prophet, "I have spoken with the prophets, I granted many visions; by means of the prophets likenesses were made of me." (Hos 12:10 LXX) Accordingly, when Ezekiel made prostration to God sitting on the throne above the chariot in the likeness of a man, he was making prostration only to a likeness, as we said. But the likeness was an icon.

CHAPTER XII

Abstract: A refutation of those who say that the icons to which the Christians make prostration have no contact with that of which they are the icon, in the way in which the likeness that Ezekiel saw was in contact with God. Names and icons are equivalent in the indicative function; whatever contempt or honor is shown to names or icons makes contact with that to which the icons or names point.

If anyone says that the icons to which the Christians make acts of prostration have no contact with that of which they are the icons, as did the likenesses I have mentioned, in which God appeared to the prophets, he should understand that neither were the ark of the Lord's holiness, nor the other utensils of the tent of testimony in contact with that of which they were the icons or the representations. Yet they were shown the highest honor, as we have explained.

If you want to understand that God made representations with no obvious connection, by means of which what one would do with them would make the contact with that of which they were the representations and images, listen to what he says to Moses:

> You shall take two stones of emerald and engrave on them the names of the sons of Israel, six on one stone, and six on the other stone, according to their names. A craftsman in stone work engraves signets; you shall engrave the two stones with the names of the sons of Israel. You shall set the two stones on the shoulders of the cloak, here a stone and there a stone, as a memorial for the sons of Israel. Let Aaron carry the names of the sons of Israel on his shoulders before the Lord as a memorial for their cause. (Exod 28:9-12)

A little further on God says to Moses:

> You shall make the robe of judgment a variously colored one, like the manufacture of the cloak, clearly squared off. You shall spread out four rows of stones, and you shall put their names on the stones of each row. (Exod 28:15-17)

Then he says: "For the names of the sons of Israel, let the stones be twelve — according to the names of their twelve tribes." (Exod 28:21)

Then he says:

> Let Aaron carry the names of the sons of Israel on the robe of judgment, on his breast, when he enters into the sanctuary before the Lord.... And so shall Aaron bring in the judgment of the sons of Israel on his breast in front of the Lord forever. (Exod 28:29-30)

Evidently the Lord, the knower of all things before their coming to be, in his condescension wanted the names of the sons of Israel as a memorial before him, as if the sons of Israel, at the sight of their names would be standing in his presence beseeching him, and in his mercy he would be favorably disposed toward them, even though these names had no real connection with the sons of Israel. So how can the Christians be blamed for making icons of the face of Christ in the course of carrying out his ministry, or of the faces of the saints in the entanglement of their affairs, as memorials to motivate them to express gratitude to the Messiah for having become incarnate for the sake of their salvation, and to emulate the saints in what they endured for the love of him? To look at the icons of them, even if the icons have no contact with them, is like looking at them themselves.

If someone says that names are not like icons, he is only speaking out of his ignorance of the facts. The fact is that he does not understand that written names are representations, or figures for sounds, and the sounds are representations for ideas, and ideas are representations for things, as the philosophers say. So then, are not the icons simply a clear writing that anyone can understand, whether he can read or he cannot read? Consequently, in a way they are better than writing, because both writing and icons are memorials for the things to which they point, but in functioning as memorials, the icons are much more eloquent than writing for their purpose of instructing someone who cannot read — on the grounds that for instruction they are more reliable than writing.

The surprise of the dullness of the Jews and others is at their reproach of the Christians for their honoring of the icons of the saints, even though they have no real contact with the saints, since these people are not ashamed of doing the same thing for which they reproach the Christians. Let the Jew, or anyone else who lays claim to faith, advise us. Suppose a man writes on a piece of paper the name of God's friend, Abraham, or of God's prophets, Isaac, Jacob, Moses, or David. Then someone inimical to these holy prophets gets the piece of paper, spits on it, tramples it underfoot and dirties it, out of enmity for these prophets. would not the perpetrator of this deed in their eyes be deserving of death, as if he had done it to the prophets in person? Here is something about which there is no doubt. It is understood that the names have no real contact with the prophets. Nevertheless, it would be sufficient, if they knew it, for them to show honor to that piece of paper, to hold it in high regard, and to treat it with respect.

If icons are better than writing, as we have explained, then in that respect they are ahead of names. Therefore, in making prostration to the icons of the saints, not by way of adoration but by way of the honor the saints deserve from all the believers, the Christians are but making prostration to the saints in person. And this is enough to justify the Christians' practice of making prostration to the icons of the saints.

CHAPTER XIII

Abstract: Testimony from the prophets that icons are equivalent to writing, and that it is what one does with icons or names that makes the contact with that to which the names or icons belong.

If you want to know from God's word that icons are equivalent to writing in functioning as memorials, listen to how he speaks in Isaiah the prophet:

> Sion said the Lord has abandoned me, and the Lord has forgotten me. Does a woman then forget her baby? Does she not have compassion for the child of her womb? But even if the woman forgets him, I shall never forget you, says the Lord. I have drawn an icon of your walls on my hands; you are before me forever. You will be rebuilt faster than they pulled you down, and your tormentors will depart from you. (Isa 49:14-17)

Evidently, just as the names of the sons of Israel engraved on the stones used to remind the Lord to have compassion on them, so too the icon of Sion that the Lord drew on his hands reminded him of Sion — to have compassion on her, and to bring her inhabitants back to her. He used to look at Sion, but only in her icon.

Therefore, truly we say that the Christians, when they make prostration to the icons of the saints, they are but making prostration to the saints themselves. Likewise, if someone shows either contempt or honor to the names of the prophets written on the piece of paper, they are but showing contempt or honor to the prophets themselves. And just as anyone who would show contempt to these names should in justice be deserving of death, so also anyone of the Christians who shows contempt to the icons of the saints deserves spiritual death; anyone who honors them is without a doubt entitled to everlasting life.

Again, if you want to know from God's word that icons and writing are equivalent, and that it is what one does with icon or writing that makes the contact with that which they indicate, in the way we mentioned at the beginning, listen to how God speaks to the prophet Ezekiel:

> You, O man, take for yourself a brick and set it in front of you. Trace on it the city of Jerusalem, and then encircle her, and build a bulwark against her; dig a trench, encamp armies against her, and station a catapult in her vicinity. Then take for yourself an iron plate, a wall of iron between you and the city, and set the likeness of your face against her, so that she will be under siege; invest her. This is a sign for the sons of Israel. (Ezek 4:1-3)

Evidently the prophet made an icon of the city before him, in the way God told him. Everything done to her icon made contact with her; the like of it was done to her, as it was in the icon.

As for writing, it is equivalent to the icon in this respect. What one does with it is what makes the contact with that which it indicates, just as what one does with the icon makes the contact with that of which it is the icon. In Jeremiah the prophet the following is written:

> The word that God commanded Jeremiah the prophet to speak to Seriah, the son of Neriah, the son of Mahseriah, when Zedekiah the king of Judah sent him to Babylon with gifts, in the fourth year of his reign. Jeremiah wrote down all the trials that would come upon Babylon, all the words about Babylon written in a single book. And he said to Seriah, "When you come to Babylon, read this book and these words, and say,"O Lord, you have said about this place that you will uproot it, and no dweller will remain in it, of men or of beasts, and it will be ruined forever." When you finish reading this book, tie up a stone in it and throw it into the middle of the Euphrates, and you shall say,"So shall Babylon be submerged in the trials that have come upon her, says the Lord"." (Jer 51:59-64)

Just as what was done with this piece of writing made the contact with Babylon, and the like of it was done to her; so also what the prophet Ezekiel did with her icon made the contact with Jerusalem[97].

CHAPTER XIV

Abstract: Whoever makes prostration to a saint's icon rouses the saint to pray to God in his behalf. The saints are intermediaries between God and man; in both their life and their death they make him pleased with man.

Here is the proof that when the Christians make prostration to the icons of the saints, intending thereby to honor the saints, it is only their prostration of honor that provides the contact with the saints themselves. Whoever honors the saints, no doubt deserves the greatest reward from the God of the saints. And the saints become his representatives at God's gate. They raise up his prayers, strengthen them, and ask for their fulfillment from the Lord in his behalf. For God in his goodness has made the saints intermediaries between himself and his worshippers, for the sake of honoring the saints, and for the sake of exciting the interest of others in enjoying with him what they enjoy. He sometimes gets angry with his servants, and refuses them a favor until the saints call upon him.

[97] The insistence on the idea that what one does with an icon is what makes the contact between the icon and the person whom the icon represents is one of Abū Qurrah's contributions to the developing theology of the icons. His thinking on the subject may be said to be "functionalist", even liturgical, rather than "essentialist". In this respect there are comparisons to be made with the thought of Theodore the Studite. See C. P. Roth (trans.), *St. Theodore the Studite on the Holy Icons* (Crestwood, N.Y., 1981).

For this there are many testimonies. Who does not know that God was angry at the Israelites when they worshipped the calf, and he wanted to exterminate them? So Moses went up to him, with the result that he deflected him from his anger and made him pleased with them. God said to him, "I have become pleased with them only because of you." (see Exod 32:11-14)

Who does not know that God barely mentioned the affair of Sodom to Abraham, when it occurred to him to plead with him in their behalf? Truly it was due to Abraham that graciousness could come to her people.

Then there was the prophet Elijah; did God not give him such power to close and to open the heavens as if he had released to him something of [the divine] economy? God gave him the authorization, and he did not annul his holy prophet's word. Rather, he carried out his decisions, and people came to beseech not him but his prophet, blessed by his majesty. (see 1 Kgs 17:1; 18:1, 41-46)

The magnanimity [of God] has surpassed all imagination, that he should withhold his mercy from his servants until his friends would elicit it from him for them, as if he were making praise for his loved ones as much of a requirement as it is for himself, and even more! Not only during the lifetime of his loved ones does he do this for them, but even after their demise he makes people's honor for them continue to the point that it is through them they gain access to him. How many times is it mentioned in the scriptures that good was done on account of Abraham, Isaac, and Jacob — after their demise! How often after their time has an intercession been made through them! How often, after David's death, was Jerusalem saved on account of David! This is well known to anyone who reads the scripture.

Therefore, great profit is at the disposal of the Christians, on the occasion of their making the act of prostration to the icons of the saints, since it is this action that puts them into contact with the saints. By my life, no one can walk up to a saint's icon and make the prostration before it without rousing the saint whose image it is to pray on one's behalf. Nor does the one making the prostration care that not much speaking is required along with his prostration. By my life, the saint knows better than he does what will benefit him. This is a great blessing which the one who makes a prostration acquires effortlessly. Who would not covet it?

After God, should we not want to bring forward the example of earthly kings: how one gives honor to his companions, his door-keepers, his ministers, and the people of preference in his entourage? These people act as one's proxies at the king's door, securing one's needs for him, in his absence or in his presence.

CHAPTER XV

Abstract: The tablets of the Law were shown the greatest honor, because of the Lord's handwriting that was set down on them; they were an icon for the incarnation of the Word God.

How can anyone forget the greatest, the most famous icon, the tablets of the Law which were put into the ark of the Lord, on which there were engraved by the Lord's finger the ten words the Lord addressed to the Israelites? Was this not simply the icon of the actual Word of God, which was to become incarnate from the Holy Spirit and from the virgin Mary at the end-time?

The actual Word of God was simply likened to ten words because the Word of God is hypostatically perfect, and the number "ten" is the most perfect of all numbers, because numbering begins from "one," goes up until it reaches "ten," then it comes back to "one" and revolves on itself indefinitely. God's finger is known to be the Holy Spirit; when Christ our Lord says in the Gospel, "By the finger of God I drive out devils," (Luke 11:20), another Evangelist provides the explanation, and gives in the same place as a quotation of Christ's saying, "By the Spirit of God I drive out devils." (Matt 12:28) The ark of the Lord is Mary, in whom the Word of God dwelt incarnate, who was divinized. Sin did not impair her, just as the ark was of unimpaired wood, covered with gold inside and out. But here is not the place where it is appropriate for us to give a summary of the referents of these icons, or to trace them back to their models, of which one is well aware[98].

Due to their coarsemindedness, the Jews think what we have to say of these signs is babble. Woe be to them, they do not understand that since it has been proved in regard to these things that they are icons for other things, — when God said to Moses, "Make everything a representation of the model I showed you on the mountain," (see Exod 25:40) — they do then have referents and meanings. And they do not refer to a meaning more estimable than Christ's economy, which is the utmost hope for them and for us; all prophecy, in the aggregate of its modes, discloses it and points to it.

Because the matter is as we have said, that God's speech figured on the tablets was but an icon for the incarnation of Christ, the eternal Word of God, the prophets accordingly used to bow down in prostration in its presence; the Levites used to make prostration in front of it; the cloud of the Lord's honor used to frequent it. For this reason David said, "Arise, O Lord, to your rest, you and the ark of your holiness." (Ps 132:8)

[98] Note the conjunction of typology and iconography that lies behind this paragraph, something Abū Qurrah takes for granted. See André Grabar, *Christian Iconography; a Study of its Origins* (Princeton, 1968), pp. 137 ff.

Do you think, O Jew, there was an act of levitation in the ark
that was of wood at the moment of someone's bidding it to rise?
No! Rather, it was a reference to the angel's saying to Joseph in
Bethlehem, "Rise, take the boy and his mother and flee into
Egypt... Herod will seek him out to kill him." (Matt 2:13) So the
incarnate Word of God got up, he and the ark of his holiness,
who is Mary, and fled to his rest in Egypt, away from the outrage
of the Jews against him, and their search to kill him. David had
mentioned Bethlehem in this connection in his saying, "We heard
of it in Ephrathah." (Ps 132:6) And here is the prophet Isaiah's
statement: "The Lord is riding on a swift cloud, entering Egypt."
(Isa 19:1)

If you doubt that these inanimate things are icons for living
reality, how are we to deal with Joshua, son of Nun? He took a big
stone and set it up under the terebinth, in front of the Lord. He
said to the sons of Israel:

> This will be for a testimony for you, because it has heard everything
> said to you today from the Lord. And it will be for a testimony for
> you in later days, when you will have disowned the Lord, your
> God. (Jos 4:4-9)

Do you think, O Jew, this stone heard the Lord's speech and
testified for him in later days against the sons of Israel? It would
be sheer madness if it were not an icon to signify some other, living, hearing, testifying being.

Therefore, it is like what we said about the words that were
inscribed on the two tablets; they are an icon for the incarnation
of the eternal Word of God. Is not writing only an icon for audi-
ble speech? So, this is an icon for the primordial, talking Word, as
we said at the outset.

No one should be surprised at the Jew when he does not understand these things, because he is coarse and stupid, as the prophets

have testified about him; blindness is deep-seated in his heart. As St. Paul said, "Until today, when the old commandment is read, coarseness prevails over their hearts." (Rom 11:8) Rather, the surprise is that there are insane Christians turning away from the making the offer of prostration to the icon of Christ, and to the icons of the saints. These people do not doubt that the icon we have authenticated from the Old [Testament] accords with the interpretation we have given it. They think the old icon is worth the utmost honor, yet they are the ones fleeing from paying honor to the holy icons!

CHAPTER XVI

Abstract: Because of the dullness of the ancients, God used to discharge his mysteries among them only by means of such miracles as their eyes could see in connection with them. Christians do not need anything like this. Nevertheless, for the sake of the outsiders, and the lowest rank of the Christians, God continues to manifest miracles in behalf of the mysteries of Christianity, and in behalf of the strong relationship of the icons with those of whom they are the icons.

If these Christians should say that to pay honor to the tablets [of the Law] evidently was of God, since the cloud of his honor used to come down upon them, as it is written in the book of Kings (see 1 Kgs 8:10-11), whereas we do not see anything of the sort pertaining to the icons that are in churches, we say to them that due to the dullness of the ancients, God's mysteries were never grand in their estimation, unless they could see their grandeur with their own eyes. For this reason, when the first offerings were offered in the Tent of Testimony, a fire came down upon them (Lev 9:24), and even upon the offering which was offered in the temple of Jerusalem when Solomon built it (2 Chr 7:1).

As for us Christians, who have been given discernment in the Holy Spirit, we have no need for this sort of thing. Therefore, when our Lord gave his body and blood to his disciples in the upper room in Jerusalem, he handed over to them only bread and wine. He said to them, "This is my body and my blood." (Mark 14:22-24; Matt 26:26-28) And their minds penetrated to the certainty in his speech, without seeing any glory manifested over what he handed to them. This same practice continues among the Christians; they offer the offering, knowing for certain that it is Christ's body and blood, without seeing after the consecration anything except what they put forward before it was consecrated.

As in the case of the rest of the mysteries, so must the holy icons, equivalent to the other items, receive honor comparable to the honor accorded to them, even though nothing of dread or splendor appears in connection with them. Nevertheless, for the sake of the outsiders, or because of the dullness of the lowest class of Christians in religious observance, God has in fact often manifested the glory of the mysteries of Christianity, as we hear everyday, from those stories about which the mind can have no doubt once it has dealt honestly with them.

As St. Athanasius said above, he is seen in the bones of the saints, and their icons[99]. And we ourselves see the benefits of the oil that flows from their bones; it cures illnesses that surpass

---

[99] See chap. VIII above. The writer does not in fact say this in the passage Abū Qurrah quotes from the *Quaestiones ad Antiochum Ducem*.

human medicine. Many people have seen demons tormented in front of their tombs, and vehemently expelled.

In our own day there was a well-known martyr, from a family of the highest nobility among the outsiders, whose story is widespread. May he remember us to Christ in his prayers, he is called St. Anthony. He used to tell everyone he met that he came to believe in Christianity only because of a miracle he saw in connection with an icon that belonged to St. Theodore, the martyr[100].

There is also the icon that the Jews once produced in their city, Tiberias, when they made an icon of Christ crucified, so they could mock him. One of them stabbed the icon with a lance, and blood and water ran out of it. Then a blind man who was present came up to it; because of his good intention the Holy Spirit had cast faith into his heart. He said to them, "Put my hand on the spot of the stab-wound, so that I too can take part with you in the stabbing." When they put his hand there, he wiped off some of the blood and water, and smeared it over his eyes, so that they were opened. Then he took what he could of this boon and carried it off to various places. In these places it became the endowment of monasteries and churches; in them miracles occurred on account of the godsend (*al-barakah*), as we hear from many people, both outsiders and Christians. One of these monasteries in the district of Aleppo is named the monastery of St. Ananias, after the name of the believing Jew bore who brought the godsend (*al-barakah*) and the story of the icon we mentioned, well-known and famous in all the churches of the Christians[101].

---

[100] See Ignace Dick, "La passion arabe de s. Antoine Ruwaḥ, néomartyr de Damas (=25 déc. 799)," *Le Muséon* 74 (1961), pp. 109-133. See also Kotter, *Contra Imaginum Calumniatores*, p. 184 for another story about the mutilation of the icon of St. Theodore.

[101] Six versions of a similar story are among the spurious works attributed to St. Athanasius in PG, vol. XXVIII, cols. 797-824. See also the Syriac account,

One should not be surprised at our saying that icons deserve honor, and that we see Christ and the saints in the icons of them at which we look, since we hear St. Paul saying that the icons are the very realities themselves. For example, in reference to the rock from which water burst forth for the Israelites (Exod 17:6; Num 20:11), there is his saying that it was Christ (1 Cor 10:4). One knows that this rock was not Christ himself, but it was an icon for Christ. Likewise in connection with Christ, the Evangelist said that it is written, "Not a bone of him shall be broken" (John 19:36). This was written only about the lamb that the Israelites had sacrificed in Egypt at the Passover (Exod 12:46), which was an icon for Christ.

This is a sufficient justification, from the Old [Testament] and the New [Testament], for the act of prostration in the way of honor that the icons of the saints deserve. It would be better for anyone of the Christians not satisfied with it to become a Jew, due to the dullness of his mind.

CHAPTER XVII

Abstract: A rebuke to the Jew; he too is commanded to make prostration to something other than God. Moreover, due to his honoring a stone, it is also incumbent upon him to make prostration to the four rivers coming out of Paradise, and to make his prostration in the direction of the sun.

"The History of the Likeness of Christ, and of how the Accursed Jews in the City of Tiberias made a Mock thereof in the Days of the God-Loving Emperor Zeno," in E. A. Wallis Budge, *The History of the Blessed Virgin Mary and the History of the Likeness of Christ* (2 vols.; London, 1899), vol. II, p. 171 ff.

As for you, O Jew, you who maintain that one must not make prostration except to God, remaining attached to God's word to you, you are the one who has not understood its meaning, nor will you ever understand it as long as you remain a Jew. What do you make of David the prophet? He commands you to make prostration to the Lord's footstool (Ps 99:5). Because you do not comprehend the spiritual meaning of scripture, for you it must be the earth. As the Lord said in Isaiah the prophet, "The heavens are my throne, and the earth is my footstool." (Isa 66:1) So it is incumbent on you from this quotation to make prostration to the very earth. Will you in the meantime sneer at the Christians for their practice of making prostration to the icons of Christ and his saints, when you are found to be making prostration to every bit of dirt in the dustbin?

As for your devotion to the rock that is in Jerusalem, were you allowed access to it, whoever can read will know that you would kiss it and anoint it when you would arrive, and this to honor it[102]. So, to make prostration to it is incumbent upon you, since you have been given proof that the act of prostration is sometimes by way of honor.

But tell us what gives you an obligation toward this rock? I know you will say that it came from the Garden, and therefore one makes an effort to honor it. But your saying it came from the Garden is not a proof of it, because there is no mention of it in

---

[102] Abū Qurrah must be referring to the *'eben shetiyyah* over which the caliph ʿAbd al-Malik (685-705) built the Dome of the Rock. See O. Grabar, "*Ḳubbat al-Sakhra,*" *EI*, new ed., vol. V, pp. 298-299, with further bibliography. According to the report of some fourth century pilgrims to the Holy Land from Bordeaux, Jews used to come yearly to the stone to anoint it, and to conduct mourning ceremonies there. See the discussion and bibliography in Th. A. Busink, *Der Tempel von Jerusalem von Salomo bis Herodes* (2 vols.; Leiden, 1970 & 1980), vol. I, p. 6 and vol. II, pp. 904-914.

any of your prophets. Nevertheless, since you judge it to be a duty to pay every honor to this rock because, as you say, it comes from the Garden, we should press your judgment of duty upon you. In that case, honor and make prostration to the Euphrates and the Tigris, and to the other two rivers of which scripture says that they come from the Garden (Gen 2:10-14).

Even before this passage, there is one to oblige you to make your prostration only toward the east, because the Garden was in the east, as the Torah says, "God planted a garden in Eden, in the east." (Gen 2:8)[103]

CHAPTER XVIII

Abstract: An explanation of the reason why God denounced the practice of making prostration to images, and publicly said, "You shall not make prostration to them, etc." (Exod 20:5)

Perhaps some Christian will say, "Why in the Old [Testament] did God denounce this prostration and publicly say,"Do not make likenesses for yourself, nor make prostration to them, nor worship them?"(see Exod 20:4-5; Deut 5:8-9) To him we say that the Israelites had gone mad about worshipping idols. If God had forthrightly given them permission to make prostration to images, they would have used God's word as a pretext, and they would have run wild in worshipping idols.

Rather, God simply dealt with them like the wise parent deals with a headstrong, ignorant son he might have; he knows about him that if he gets control of a sword he will hit his brothers and

---

[103] The point of Abū Qurrah's remark is that the Christian *qiblah* is eastward.

the household people with it. A king would want his son to gain a mastery of the sword, to fight his enemies with it. But he knows that if the sword is put into his hand he will only hit the people of his own household with it. So he gives the order that he is not even to hold a sword in his hand at all.

So it is with God; due to his knowledge of the fact that the Israelites had no aptitude to make distinctions in their prostration to images, to steer it into the right way, away from the wrong way, he prohibited them from making prostration to any image. In his holy scriptures he secretly affirmed the practice of making prostration, until the Christians would come, who were gifted with intelligence and subtlety of mind in the Holy Spirit. They would probe into the practice, recognize it, and worship with it. As the angel said to the prophet Daniel, "O Daniel, conceal the words and seal the book until the end of time, until many will come to know, and knowledge will increase." (Dan 12:4) This is the reason God prohibited the Israelites from making prostration to any images, in the literal sense of the word, which someone with no intelligence could understand strictly.

The apostles recognized this fact; they gave permission for the icons to become customary in the Christians' churches. They could be honored, and one could make prostration to them, in recognition of the fact that no one feared for the Christians what was feared in the instance of the Israelites.

God dealt in the same way with the Israelites in regard to food stuffs, in that he gave them prohibitions, and declared many items unlawful for them. For them he put the name "unclean" on these things, to make the items odious to them under this name, so that they would avoid them. For appetite was overpowering to them; they were like dogs, having no control over themselves, to hold themselves back from their desires. Such did God name them in

Isaiah the prophet, "They are impudent dogs, knowing no satiety; they are evil, recognizing no intelligence; all of them follow their own ways." (Isa 56:11)

Clearly God, in his wisdom, affixed the name "unclean" to something of his creation, disposing matters in such a way as was suitable to the Israelites, commensurate with their dullness. He publicly used the label "unclean" in the commandment by which he instructed them. But it is well known that in what God created there is nothing unclean. As it says in the Torah, "God saw everything he had created, and it was very good" (Gen 1:31). What is good is not unclean. As St. Paul said, "Everything God created is good. Nothing is prohibited when a man takes it with praise and thanksgiving". (1 Tim 4:4)

Just as God prohibited these things and for the sake of the Israelites publicly called them unclean, and kept their cleanness and their legitimacy secret in his scriptures, to be understood in his own time, so among these same people did he publicly call the act of prostration to images an abominable practice. He made its goodness obscure in his scriptures, as we explained, for the sake of the learning of the Christians, who were to be given the Holy Spirit, which was not given to these people. As our Lord says in the Gospel, "Whoever believes in me, as scripture says, from within him rivers of living water shall flow. (By this he means the Spirit, which those who would believe in him would receive; whereas the Spirit was still not given, because Jesus was still not glorified)." (John 7:38-39)

God restrained the Israelites' practice of prostration, and their worship; he did not let it go out of bounds in public, in accord with him saying, "To the Lord your God shall you make prostration; him alone shall you worship." (Deut. 6:13, as in Matt 4:10) God kept Son and Spirit secret, each one of them perfect God like him, of his being, like him deserving prostration, so that this practice might not become a pretext for them to accept gods along with God — due to their mania for worshipping many gods and making prostration to them. He concealed the knowledge of this reality in all his scriptures, to become evident in his own good time.

As for the Christians, he declared it to them plainly, in the most public voice: God has a Son and a Spirit, each one of which is God like God, and of his very being. So they worship the Son and the Spirit together with God, but they do not worship many gods. Rather, they say that God, and his Son, and his Spirit, are one God because their minds have the subtlety to understand this matter, since the Holy Spirit flowed into them at the crucifixion of Christ, which is his glory, as we have said. Therefore, no one should deny it to God, that he forbade the Israelites publicly to make prostration to any image whatever, for the reason we have cited, but he inspired the apostles to give permission for it to the Christians, about whom no one fears what used to be feared for those others. What Christian have you ever seen adoring any of these icons? God forbid!

As for the Israelites, they adored the bronze serpent that Moses made in the desert. They offered incense to it until king Hezekiah abolished it, as it says in the book of Kings (2 Kgs 18:4). Moses and those after him had left it as a memorial, so that glory might be given to God on account of it; in the desert the Israelites had been saved from lethal snake bite by looking at it (Num 21:9). So the Israelites were allowed to give God glory by means of it; but in their error they adored it, even though they had been given the strongest prohibition against making prostration to or adoring any likeness or image. So how would it have been, had they been given an even broader concession in this matter?

Here is just a little bit of the enormous amount of material in the Holy Scriptures to show that God provided this sort of injunction to the Israelites, only in proportion to what they could accommodate at that time, not in conformity with the truth according to his will. For example, in the matter of divorce, which had been permitted to them by Moses, he said to their scribes:

> Moses allowed this to them only because of the hardness of their hearts. From the beginning it was not so. Rather, God made them male and female, and he said, "Let a man leave his father and his mother and cleave to his wife, and let the two of them become one flesh." And he said, "What God has put together, let man not put asunder." (Mark 10:5-9)

CHAPTER XIX

Abstract: Additional proof for this line of reasoning, from scripture and from analogous issues of reason.

An indication that things are as we have said — namely, that God simply adjusted these commandments to the Israelites, not as he himself willed, but according to what they could bear — is his saying in the prophet Ezekiel, "I gave them commandments that were not good, and statutes by which they could not live" (Ezek 20:25). Just prior to this passage he says, "They did not accomplish my commandments, nor did they keep my statutes, by which anyone who keeps them lives" (Ezek 20:21). Can you not clearly see him saying about his commandments that they are not good, and about his statutes both that no one lives by them, but that one might live by them?

In his dealings with the Israelites, God resembles nothing so much as a king who had a son who was so impassioned about

games he was unable to restrain himself, not because he was incapable of doing so, but because of the slackness of his desire. He used
to play with knives, and his father was afraid that one day he would
be hit by a knife and it would kill him. But the boy could not bear
to be forbidden to play altogether. For this reason his father would
say to him, "Son, do not play with a knife, play with a ball." Then
he would extol the advantages of ball-playing in his eyes, and try to
make it attractive to him. One knows that the father's will for the
son was not that he play ball, but that he would give up playing
entirely, to give himself to literature, philosophy, and important,
useful things. This tactic of the father toward the son is not a right
definition of reality. The son will put it aside when his mind reaches
maturity. In such a way did God deal with the Israelites.

Therefore, it is not right for the "beasts" among us Christians,
those who will not make prostration to the icons of the saints, to
allege against us God's saying to the Israelites, "Do not make for
yourself a likeness of anything in the heavens, or on earth, or in
the waters; do not make prostration to it, nor worship it." (Deut
5:8-9) For, his declaration in public of the ignobility of making
prostration to these likenesses is like his declaration in public of
the ignobility of the animals he prohibited; he maintained that
they were unclean, and that they were too defiled to eat. But in
his scriptures he had also made it clear to intelligent people that
there is nothing unclean in all creation; he showed them that he
put the name "unclean" on what he prohibited, only for a certain
purpose, not because it was really unclean.

Accordingly, in his scriptures he made it plain to the discerning, that to make prostration to an icon, the prostration it
deserves, is good, as we have proved. He made them understand
that he pronounced it to be repulsive, and prohibited it, only for
a certain purpose, not because it was really repulsive.

If the Jew says God does not prohibit the permitted, nor does he name the permitted "unclean," we shall throw his own judgment back against him. We say to him, the prohibited should not then be permitted, nor should the prohibited be named "good," what he called abominable for you, and designated as unclean, if he did not understand it to be the uncleanness of which we speak? He would not, blessed be he, have been consistent in either understanding or speech. Rather, he would only be vacillating in both word and knowledge. Far be it from him for it to be so!

But what we say is true; he only declared certain animals ignoble, and he declared the practice of making prostration to likenesses ignoble, not because they deserved the declaration of ignobility on his part, but by reason of the dispensation of which we spoke in connection with the Israelites and their childishness. As St. Paul said in his epistle to them:

> You have become hard of hearing. You should be teachers, because you have spent so much time. But now you need to learn the A B C's of God's word; milk has come to be what will agree with you, not solid food; it is suitable for mature people, whose bodies have come to have senses capable of distinguishing the good from the bad. (Heb 5:11-14)

So, the Israelites remained children after an age-long detention in instruction. How could it not be right for God to have conversed with them only as one would converse with children, in stories that appeal to them? It is like a mother, when she wants to wean her child from her milk; she gives the milk ugly names. It is not because it deserves such names, but to put the child off it and to turn him away from it, because at the stage of life in which he is, it is not appropriate for him.

Similarly, God attached ugly names to the practice of making prostration to the icons, and to the animals he prohibited, not because of their deserts, but because they were not appropriate for the Israelites at that time in their lives. When maturity came, Christ our Lord spoke clearly in his Gospel, to the contrary of what he said in the Law. He said to the people at large, "It is not what goes into the mouth that defiles a man." (Matt 15:11) And he allowed the apostles to make prostration to the icons; he disclosed what had been hidden in enigmas from the common people among the ancients.

We think we have gone on long enough with testimonies from the Holy Scriptures, and with the study of them, to justify the practice of making prostration to the holy icons. The only harm in this would be if we were to leave out some passage an adversary could allege, without our having cited it here, and we would have thereby given rise to an embarrassment. The result is that no distress at this practice of prostration, of which the advantage is so great, should befall any Christian.

CHAPTER XX

Abstract: A rebuttal to whomever it is who says that God has the authority to command this or that, while it is inappropriate for people to differ publicly with God's word, unless he has commanded them to do it.

At the outset we declared that even though God publicly commanded the Israelites not to make any likeness, he commanded Moses to make two Cherubim and the serpent [of bronze]. (Exod 25:18; Num 21:8-9) Thereby he showed that for his part the prohibition was only an exercise of *oikonomia*, according to his will's design[104].

---

[104] The Arabic word Abū Qurrah uses here, *at-tadbīr*, is the standard Arabic term used to translate the Greek word *oikonomia*, "economy," which as a theo-

Someone might say that God has the authority to command this or that, but it does not belong to men to do anything contrary to what God has commanded, unless he so commands them. We say to this person that God publicly commanded that no one should make prostration to anyone other than to him. But the prophets made prostrations to people without God personally commanding them to make prostration to the people, because they understood the meaning of his statement in the prohibition.

Solomon, David's son, provided many images for the house which he built for God in Jerusalem: Cherubim, fruit, lions etc., without God's express command to provide them. In the book of Chronicles it says David gave Solomon a model of the house and of the things he prescribed for it. (1 Chr 28:11-19) Rather, he described the model to him according to the capacity of his intelligence. These two prophets did what they did, only because they understood the meaning of God's saying that no likeness of anything was to be made; they knew that it was not by itself according to the design of his will.

David even ate the bread that used to be set before the Lord, which no one except the priests had the authority to eat, unless God would command someone to eat it. (1 Sam 21:5-7) The Maccabees allowed fighting for life on the Sabbath day, without God's giving them any command about it. (1 Macc 2:41) But it would not be right for anyone to say that David and the Maccabees used to grant a release from God's command, or used to violate it out

logical expression was used by early Christian writers in a variety of ways, including the sense of that "accommodation" or "disposition," even "dispensation," by which God in his providence governed the ordering of salvation history. See B. Studer, "Economy," in Angelo Di Berardino (ed.), *Encyclopedia of the Early Church* (2 vols.; Cambridge, 1992), vol. I, p. 262. See also K. Duchatelez, "La notion d'économie et ses richesses théologiques," *Nouvelle Revue Théologique* 92 (1970), pp. 267-308

of coercion. By my life, Antiochus, the Greek king (Antiochus IV Epiphanes, 175-164 B.D.), pressed the seven Maccabees and their elderly teacher Eleazar; he ordered all kinds of tortures for them, to make them eat pork, but they refused and died under torture. (2 Macc 6:18-7:41)

Rather, the holy men granted a release from the legal injunction concerning the bread, and concerning the observance of the Sabbath, only in recognition of the fact that God publicly gave the command to the masses only as an exercise in *oikonomia*, not because for his part it was absolute. Christ confirmed their understanding with his abolition of this bread and of the observance of the Sabbath.

The Sabbath was a delight for the masses of the Jews, as it says in Isaiah, the prophet. (Isa. 58:13) But Moses, Elijah, and Daniel, instead of a delight, made of the Sabbath a day of fasting: the first one of them went hungry twice for forty days (Exod 24:18 & Deut 9:25); the second one went hungry for forty days once (1 Kgs 19:8); the third one went hungry for twenty-one days (Dan 10:2). So these three prophets acted at variance with the position of the Law for the general populace, without God giving them any command to do it, because of an understanding of the meaning of God's word. He made the Sabbath a delight for the Jews, by reason of their bellies' appetite, only so that it might lead them to observe it, and that in their observance of it they might come to know their God, the creator of heaven and earth, and not worship anything else. As it says in the Torah, on the occasion of the Israelites' Exodus,

> God spoke to Moses, and he said to him, "Give the Israelites a command; say to them, "See that you keep my Sabbaths. They are a sign between me and you for age after age, so that you might know that I am the Lord, the one who sanctifies you". (Exod 31:12-13)

A little further on he says,

> Let the Israelites observe my Sabbaths... It is a covenant forever
> between me and the Israelites; it is a sign forever that in six days the
> Lord created heaven and earth, and on the seventh day he rested.
> (Exod 31:16-17)

Once again, Elijah acted at variance with the Law in his setting
up of a sacrifice to God somewhere other than in the temple at
Jerusalem, and in his preparation of it in a manner other than the
one prescribed in the Law (1 Kgs 18:30-35), without God commanding him to do it, because of his recognition of the meaning
of God's word in the Law. He forbade the Israelites to set up a
sacrifice just any place, only because they used to make sacrifices
to demons. As it says in the book of Leviticus:

> If any Israelite man, or any one of the sojourners entering with
> them, offers a sacrifice that he did not bring to the door of the Tent
> of Testimony and then offers as a sacrifice to the Lord, that man
> deserves to be eliminated from his people. (Lev 17:8-9)
> Just previously it had said, "The Israelites shall not make their sac-
> rificial offerings to the nothings in whose train they used to go
> whoring. This is right guidance." (Lev 17:7)

Furthermore, as the scripture scholars know, God had restricted
the Israelites' sacrifices to the holy city, so that when he will have
destroyed it at the hands of the Romans, after the coming of the
Messiah, their sacrifices would be invalid, loathsome to God. So
Elijah, the prophet, with his recognition of these factors, acted at
variance with the Law by which the general populace was
directed, without God speaking to him.

Therefore, in making images and likenesses, the saints acted at
variance with the public law, "Do not make for yourself a likeness
of anything, nor make a prostration to it." (Exod 20:4-5) So what
does he have to say who maintains that God has the authority to

command this or that, and that it is not right for people publicly to act at variance with God's command without God's bidding? By my life, I have clearly shown that the saints publicly acted at variance with God's command without his bidding, due to their recognition of the reason why he gave the command. It confirms what we have been saying about the fact that prostration to the icons of the saints is incumbent upon everyone who has a knowledge of God's scriptures.

CHAPTER XXI

Abstract: A rebuttal to anyone who says to us, "Since you deem it right to make a prostration to the icon of anyone who deserves honor, make prostration to me, who am the image of God."

There are people who say that if the icons of the saints are entitled to prostration by way of honor, make prostration to me; I am, they maintain, someone who is the image of God. We say, you are someone who has spoiled God's image in yourself. God's image now only resembles the king's daughter who was the most beautiful person, whose icon was the most beautiful icon. Then a man got hold of the icon, obliterated its eyes, cut off its ears and nose, amputated its feet, severed its fingers, blackened its colors, and thoroughly spoiled it. In his possession it has become the ugliest, the most repugnant icon. Or it resembles wax on which there was the most beautiful likeness, truly representing the king's daughter, and a man took it and turned it into the likeness of a pig.

By my life, just as wax allows that the likeness on it can be changed, your nature, due to your freedom, allows you to make it an image of God, if you wish, or an image of Satan or of a beast, if you wish.

So tell me, after recognizing the king's daughter, if these [other] configurations were shown to you, would you not say they are certainly not representations of the king's daughter? The same is the case with you; without any constraint you have acted contrary to bearing a resemblance to God in your personal characteristics. In giving up among your virtues patience, self-composure, munificence, kindness, mercy, and justice, in your turning away from praiseworthy actions comparable to those we have mentioned, and in your adherence to the exact opposite, to the point that you resemble a Satan or a beast, we say to you that you are not an image for God. Therefore, we will not make prostration to you, in accord with our practice of making prostration to the saints or to their icons.

These are the ones who in themselves stand as images of God by reason of the fact that they have put off the old man with all his inconstancy, as St. Paul says, and they have put on the new one, who is renewed in the likeness of his creator. (Col 3:9-10) As for them, you see us making prostration even to their bones after their death, because they became vessels of the Holy Spirit, who does not leave them, neither in their life nor in their death.

A testimony to this is the prophet Elisha. After his death his bones raised a dead man. (2 Kgs 13:21) To this very day they are in the hands of the Christians; oil exudes from them that cures leprosy, as we have seen with our own eyes. These holy bones are in a village called Salqīn, in the district of Antioch, and elsewhere too[105].

---

[105] For Salqīn, see Claude Cahen, *La Syrie du nord à l'époque des croisades et la principauté franque d'Antioche* (Paris, 1940), pp. 153-540; Georges Tchalenko, *Villages antiques de la Syrie du nord, le massif du Bélus à l'époque romaine* (3 vols.; Paris, 1953-1958), vol. I, pp. 94-96, 421. Traditionally, Elisha's tomb was said to have been in Sebaste, Palestine, near Samaria. However, in the time of the emperor Julian the tomb was supposed to have been opened and the bones scattered to Alexandria, Constantinople and elsewhere. See *AASS*, vol. XXIII, pp. 273-275.

This matches what we have already mentioned of the miracles the saints' bones work, which we see even today. On this account intelligent people understand that the Holy Spirit resides in them.

CHAPTER XXII

Abstract: Testimony from reason that for us the status of matter, before writing or an icon is stamped on it, is not the same as its status once it has been stamped.

Here we bring to a close our refutation of the pretexts people ignorantly advance in argument from the Holy Scriptures. Now we want to unsheathe the reason to inquire into the icons, to discern if the honor or disdain with which one treats them brings joy or sorrow to those of whom they are the icons. In this connection inquirers must find out whether or not, when writing or an icon is stamped on a material substance, its status in people's eyes is the same as its status was before the writing or the icon was stamped on it.

The proof of it is the stuff on which a king might put his seal for you, in the amount of the equivalent of a hundred thousand people, against whom a sentence of death was issued. In its own right the stuff is worth nothing. When the king's seal is stamped on it for the redemption of this number of people, its value has come to surpass calculation. It is the same with a piece of paper on which the king's signature is put in the case we have mentioned.

Whoever has doubts about it should learn a lesson from the two tablets of God's law. They are two stones, but when writing was inscribed on them by the Lord's hand, they were accorded an honor by God and man, beyond which there is none more sublime.

The Torah and the Gospel are both simply written on sheets of parchment. Before God's word is written on them, sheets of parchment have no honor in anyone's eyes. But once the holy word is confirmed to be on them, they are dignified and accorded the greatest honor, to the point that were anyone to dare to burn them or to defile them out of disbelief in what is written on them, or out of disdain for it, he would deserve death from the believers for it, and this is known to everyone.

CHAPTER XXIII

Abstract: A rebuke to anyone who says of the honor or disdain with which the icon of Christ our God is treated, that the joy of it does not reach Christ in the same way as when the icon of a mother or a father is so treated among us.

Of all the icons, we will mention here the icon of Christ our God, incarnate from the virgin Mary, because in our city, Edessa "the Blest," it is honored with prostration, especially during festal seasons and pilgrimages that are its own.

If there is any Christian disinclined to make prostration to it, I would like an icon of his father to be painted at the door of the Church of the Icon of Christ. I would invite everyone who makes prostration to the icon of Christ, when he is leaving its presence, to spit in the face of the icon of this person's father, especially if his father was the one who bequeathed it to him not to make prostration to the holy icons. My purpose would be to see if he gets angry at this or not.

There can be no doubt about it; this person would be only too happy to repay anyone who did this to the icon of his father with a recompense that would go even as far as the deprivation of life in equivalency. Therefore, we say to him that if anger at the abuse of your father's icon gets to you, so that you are brought to this point, understand that so does joy at the honor paid to the icon of Christ get to him. He will repay anyone who makes prostration to it with a benefit that counterbalances the damage you are going to inflict on anyone who spits in the face of your father's icon — and even more, to the degree that his generosity is something the imagination cannot encompass.

For example, suppose there was a king whose mother was defamed among the common people because of a man who was a tramp, and the common people could recognize both the features of the king's mother and the features of the man because of whom she was defamed. Then somebody painted an icon on a panel of the king's mother engaged in sexual intercourse with that tramp, and spread the notoriety of her icon throughout the city, going around in the streets and alleys looking for an opportunity to expose her. What do you think the person's situation with the king might be? Would the king not cut him limb from limb? No doubt about it! And were the perpetrator of the deed to undertake to offer an excuse to the king, saying, "I did not do anything to your mother; I only did something with a panel and some colors," the king would get even angrier at him for his arrogance toward him and the greed in his mind.

So it suffices to say Christ our Lord, the heavenly king, will honor anyone who spreads the fame of his icon, and who makes prostration to it. Likewise, he will drive away and dismiss from his kingdom anyone who treats his icon with contempt, and who out of an arrogance of the sort we have mentioned refuses it the act of prostration.

CHAPTER XXIV

Abstract: The Christians who make icons of Christ and his saints in their churches, and who make prostration to their icons, are thereby likewise acting graciously toward Christ, and they deserve the best reward from him. Anyone of them who abandons this practice cuts himself off from what the others deserve.

Understand, my brothers, that the Christians do not act graciously toward Christ, in any other way comparable with the way they act graciously toward him with their installation of icons of him in their churches and their practice of making prostration to his icon, especially when they set up an icon of him shamefully crucified[106].

It is like a king, who ruled all the world, all of whose wise men were ignorant in comparison with his wisdom. He was the mightiest man, dressed in the most magnificent purple, whose head was crowned with a radiant crown. His beauty surpassed everything beautiful, and on-lookers would look away from his countenance. Many people were devoted to him, and they took delight in showing him love; they accorded him the highest honor.

In his wisdom, this king had in view a project he wanted, that he hid from those around him. He put on a disguise; he took off his purple, laid aside his crown, descended from his throne, and dressed in shabby, mean, vulgar clothes. Then he gave his enemies access to his position in his stead, and they beat him and treated him with a variety of humiliations. They attacked him with abuse,

---

[106] On the significance of the icon of Christ "shamefully crucified," see now the discussion and further bibliography in Anna D. Kartsonis, *Anastasis; the Making of an Image* (Princeton, 1986), pp. 40-67. See also Kathleen Corrigan, *Visual Polemics* (Cambridge, 1992).

mocking him; they were taunting him, gloating over his misfortune, and shouting at him in mockery.

When the majority of those who had sought refuge in him abandoned him dissatisfied with him, a group of them remained, who put into action their love for him, that they used to claim. They stood firmly with him in his disgrace, walking with him even though he was under the abuse of the humiliation of his enemies. And his enemies would abuse them too, saying to them, "Woe be to you, are you not ashamed to have this man as king?" And they in their turn would shout rejoicing at the top of their voices, "We have no other king, nor master, nor delight, other than this man!" So they were crucified with him, bearing his shame, and assuming a share of his sufferings, until he brought his clever project to a conclusion and returned to his kingship, and his comfortable splendor.

When this comes about, will the king not treat each one of these people correspondingly? He will spread out his whole kingdom for them and say:

> You are the ones who shared my disgrace with me, so my prosperity is open to you. By my life, you are friends in whose love there is no guile; you were the ones who used to show me honor, and in my kingdom there shall be no want of anything coming from my wealth to you. Rather, I have a whole-hearted affection [for you].

Likewise we Christians, when in our churches we install an icon of Christ shamefully crucified, and others see it, and say to us, "Woe unto you! Are you not ashamed that this is your God?" If we say at the top of our voices, "Yes indeed, he is our saviour, our hope and our joy," he will reward us for it, in proportion to his magnanimity, with a reward not lower than the reward of the martyrs, if there is no exaggeration in the statement made to those who glory in his cross and his humiliation in the presence of kings

(Gal 6:14; Matt 10:18). The esteem which we shall acquire in this matter they will lack who are annoyed by his icon and turn away from it, refusing to make prostration to it. Because of their bringing him scorn, in scorning his icon, their action will preclude them from what they would deserve from Christ, were they to bear humiliation and its consequences for his sake.

No one can deny our saying we are acting graciously toward Christ. God's scripture says, "Whoever gives to the poor makes a loan to God." (Prov 19:17) So it is likewise possible to act graciously toward him.

If anyone says that the outsiders oftentimes reproach us for the cross of Christ, without ever even seeing these icons, he should understand that were there none of these icons in our churches, what we have mentioned would never occur to the minds of most of these people going inside our churches. As for the icons, they are what arouse them to reproach us.

We who install the icons in our churches resemble a king's companions; from their knowledge of their king's excellence they glory in what is thought to be his gravest degradation, while others glory in their kings' grandest qualities. From their delight in him and the intensity of their admiration for him they trace the sign of their king's degradation on their countenances, their hands, and their clothes, in opposition to the reproach for his estate coming from those demeaning him. The disdain these people endure — that anyone should be engaging in behavior that would appear to more staid minds to be revolting, to the point that they are immersed in meanness — is what is plainer than the sun for the purpose of accommodating themselves to him. Then they will come to possess the most perfect happiness, that he in his magnanimity wants urgently to bring to all people. How much this behavior will enhance their standing with the king, no one can tell.

Therefore, blessed be anyone who makes an icon of Christ our Lord and makes prostration to his icon for the reason we have mentioned; so too anyone who makes icons of his saints and makes prostration to their icons, to honor them, to give recognition to their exploits, to seek the help of their prayers, and to be motivated to emulate them. Woe be to everyone who abandons this practice.

O Abba Yannah, our brother, accept this offering from our pitifulness. May our reward from you for our obedience to you be that you will always remember us in your prayers. Pray to Christ to make our minds fervent in the Holy Spirit. May he inspire us with an acknowledgement of the nature of his divinity and of his humanity, of the unity of his hypostasis, of the prostration due to the icon of his incarnation and to the icons of his saints. May he make us an icon for him in truth, that in ourselves here, as in a clear mirror, its outline may be perceived. And may he bring us from this world to the abode of his saints, so that with them we might one day see him face to face, and enjoy his splendor which is unflagging. To him be glory and honor, majesty and reverence, together with his Father and his immaculate Spirit, now and forever, Amen!

BIBLICAL INDEX

Qur'ānic Index